T0257167

Mac OS X Leopard
Pocket Guide

Mac OS X Leopard
Pocket Guide

Chuck Toporek

Beijing · Cambridge · Farnham · Köln · Paris · Sebastopol · Taipei · Tokyo

Mac OS X Leopard Pocket Guide

by Chuck Toporek

Published by O'Reilly Media, Inc., 1005 Gravenstein Highway North, Sebastopol, CA 95472.

O'Reilly books may be purchased for educational, business, or sales promotional use. Online editions are also available for most titles (*safari.oreilly.com*). For more information, contact our corporate/institutional sales department: (800) 998-9938 or *corporate@oreilly.com*.

Editor: Tatiana Apandi	**Cover Designer:** Karen Montgomery
Production Editor: Rachel Monaghan	**Interior Designer:** David Futato
Proofreader: Rachel Monaghan	**Illustrator:** Robert Romano
Indexer: Ellen Troutman Zaig	

Printing History:

May 2002:	First Edition.
November 2002:	Second Edition.
November 2003:	Third Edition.
June 2005:	Fourth Edition.
November 2007:	Fifth Edition.

ISBN: 978-0-596-52981-9
[TM]   [5/08]

Contents

Introduction

For the past few years, Apple has been chugging along hard and fast, revving Mac OS X at a pace nearly as fast as some of the big cats it's named for can move through the jungle. If you've been with Mac OS X from the start, you've seen Puma, Cheetah, Jaguar, Panther, and Tiger, and now we're at the next big kitty: Mac OS X Leopard (version 10.5).

Like its big-cat predecessors, Leopard brings hundreds of improvements to the Mac—things like Spotlight, the Dashboard, Automator, Safari RSS, an improved System Preferences application, tighter integration and better synchronization services with .Mac, and improved speech synthesis for accessibility. The list goes on and on. And at the system level, Apple has made a lot of refinements to the Unix layer that makes Leopard purr. For most users, those system-level changes might not mean much, but that's the way it should be. You should be able to boot your Mac, install and run software, and have a great time.

This new edition of the *Mac OS X Pocket Guide* is your quick reference to using Mac OS X Leopard. This book gives you an overview of Mac OS X Leopard, starting out by showing you what's new before providing you with a tour of the system so you can see more of what's waiting for you. Along the way, you'll learn:

- How to use Leopard's new Finder
- All about Spaces and how to quickly flip back and forth between them

- How to search for and find stuff with Spotlight
- Handy keyboard shortcuts to help you be more efficient with your Mac
- And you'll also get a bunch of quick tips for setting up and configuring your Mac to really make it your own

If you're an experienced Mac user, this book may be the only one you'll need. For Mac users coming to Mac OS X from an earlier version of the Mac OS, some of the material in this book can serve as a refresher, reminding you how to do certain things you've always been able to do on the Mac.

With more than 300 tips and tricks, this Pocket Guide is a handy reference for getting acquainted with, configuring, and working with Mac OS X Leopard.

Conventions Used in This Book

The following typographical conventions are used in this book:

Italic
: Used to indicate new terms, URLs, usernames, filenames, file extensions, Unix commands and options, program names, and directories (when viewed as a folder, the directory name is capitalized and not italicized). For example, the path in the filesystem to the Utilities folder will appear as */Applications/Utilities*.

Constant width
: Used to show the contents of files or the output from commands.

Constant width bold
: Used in examples and tables to show commands or other text that should be typed literally by the user.

Constant width italic
: Used in examples and tables to show text that should be replaced with user-supplied values; also used to show text that varies in menus.

Variable lists

The variable lists throughout this book present answers to "How do I…" questions (e.g., "How do I change the color depth of my display?"), or offer definitions of terms and concepts.

Menus/navigation

Menus and their options are referred to in the text as File → Open, Edit → Copy, etc. Arrows will also be used to signify a navigation path when using window options; for example, System Preferences → Desktop & Screen Saver → Screen Saver means you would launch System Preferences, click on the icon for the Desktop & Screen Saver preferences panel, and select the tabbed button for the Screen Saver pane within that panel.

Pathnames

Pathnames are used to show the location of a file or application in the filesystem. Directories (equivalent to folders for Mac and Windows users) are separated by forward slashes. For example, if you see something like "launch the Terminal application (*/Applications/Utilities*)" in the text, that means the Terminal application can be found in the Utilities subfolder of the Applications folder.

~

The tilde character (~) refers to the current user's Home folder. So, if you see something like *~/Library* or *~/Pictures*, that means you should go to the Library or Pictures folder, respectively, within your own Home folder. This is a much shorter representation than showing the entire path to the folder (which would be */Macintosh HD/ Users/username/Library* for the *~/Library* folder).

↵

A carriage return (↵) at the end of a line of code is used to denote an unnatural line break; that is, you should not enter these as two lines of code, but as one continuous line. Multiple lines are used in these cases due to printing constraints.

$, #

The dollar sign ($) is used in some examples to show the user prompt for the bash shell; the hash mark (#) is the prompt for the root user.

Menu symbols

When looking at the menus for any application, you will see some symbols associated with keyboard shortcuts for a particular command. For example, to open a document in Microsoft Word, you could go to the File menu and select Open (File → Open), or you could issue the keyboard shortcut, ⌘-O.

Figure P-1 shows the symbols used in the various menus to denote a keyboard shortcut.

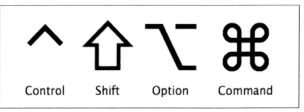

Figure P-1. These symbols are used in Mac OS X's menus for issuing keyboard shortcuts so you can quickly work with an application without having to use the mouse

Rarely will you see the Control symbol used as a menu command option; it's more often used either in association with mouse clicks to emulate a right-click on a two-button mouse or for working with the bash shell.

Safari® Books Online

When you see a Safari® Books Online icon on the cover of your favorite technology book, that means the book is available online through the O'Reilly Network Safari Bookshelf.

Safari offers a solution that's better than e-books. It's a virtual library that lets you easily search thousands of top tech books, cut and paste code samples, download chapters, and find quick answers when you need the most accurate, current information. Try it for free at *http://safari.oreilly.com*.

Acknowledgments

The past couple years has brought a lot of turmoil to my life, so I'd like to take the time to thank my family for standing by me through everything. Many thanks to my parents, and to Doug, Sheila, Boomer, and Bailey for opening their homes to me when I needed them most. Thanks for all the food and a place to crash when I needed to chill.

Thanks to the friends who stuck by me, for not letting me succumb to the madness and for always being there with a friendly ear, a shoulder to lean on, and the occasional beer to drink. Here's to the good friends who truly deserve that title. No need to mention names; when you get your copy of the book, you'll know who you are.

And finally, I'd like to thank Tatiana Apandi—one of the many unsung hero editors out there—for taking on the task of being my editor for this edition. Thanks for the vodka!

CHAPTER 1

What's New in Leopard?

Long before releasing Mac OS X Leopard, Apple offered a preview to developers and also posted some information about Leopard's top features on the Mac OS X web site (*http://www.apple.com/macosx/leopard*). But just in case you missed the big list of features, here's another rundown of what's in store for you:

- Time Machine provides a way for you to quickly, easily, and regularly back up all of the data on your Mac. Delete a file unintentionally? No worries—just launch Time Machine and you can get the file back from your last backup.

- Mail boasts new features such as integration with iCal for to-do lists, and offers a set of email templates that you can use for the messages you send.

- The new iChat features Photo Booth-like image and video features, which allow you to apply a filter to your image in video chat sessions.

- Spaces adds a new dimension to your Mac by providing you with virtual desktop spaces for managing your applications and open windows.

- Stacks lets you quickly look inside folders placed in the Dock.

- Spotlight helps you find stuff quickly and easily by indexing and cataloging content in all of the files on your system. Spotlight's search capabilities are built into the Finder, System Preferences, and many applications, including Mail and Address Book.

- iCal has received a major facelift in Leopard, and has better integration with Mail for things like To-Dos and managing appointments.

- Leopard's Accessibility features continue to be refined with things like resolution independence, in which you can zoom in on something, and the image and text will look just as crisp as they did at normal size.

- Core Animation is a new graphics programming layer that Apple provided for developers. Core Animation uses your Mac's graphics processor (known as the GPU, similar to your computer's CPU) to quickly render graphics in the user interface.

Some additional features you're bound to find useful include:

- Parental Controls lets you manage users and restrict their access to things (for example, by allowing them to view only administrator-approved web sites or controlling with whom they can chat over iChat).

- VoiceOver provides powerful accessibility features for persons with physical disabilities.

- Safari continues to improve, and with Leopard, it now supports RSS and Atom syndication protocols, automatically letting you know that a site has a news feed you can subscribe to. When you visit a web site with an RSS/Atom feed, a blue RSS icon pops up in Safari's address bar; click the RSS icon to see the site's feed.

- .Mac Sync enables you to keep valuable data on Macs, portable devices, and .Mac accounts up to date.

- Xcode 3.0 provides sweeping changes for the way programmers develop applications, allowing them to create apps more quickly and take advantage of new Apple technologies, such as Core Animation.

- More power to Unix with an improved kernel for more speed, 64-bit enhancements for Macs with Core 2 Duo and Quad Core processors.
- Changes to old standby apps like Address Book, iCal, iSync, iChat, etc.
- Lots of little enhancements and lots of big improvements, including a major overhaul to the Finder.

Whew! And that's just for starters! In total, Apple boasts more than 150 new features have been added to Mac OS X Leopard, and while some might not be so evident from the surface, you'll definitely find little gems along the way. Whether it's a vast speed improvement in Leopard's startup time or some seemingly minor new feature for your favorite application, Leopard has something to make all Mac users purr.

Cool New Features in Leopard

Here's a quick look at some of the new features added to Mac OS X Leopard.

A New Finder

So, let's get right down to it: we finally get a new, improved Finder. The Finder saw some minor changes in Mac OS X Tiger, but with Leopard, it takes on a whole new look and feel.

The Sidebar has changed (as shown in Figure 1-1), Spotlight searching has been integrated better than in the past, and new features such as Quick Look and Cover Flow have been added.

Figure 1-1. Meet Leopard's new Finder!

The new Finder is lighter, faster, better, and it totally rocks compared to the Finder in earlier versions of Mac OS X. For more information on the Finder, Quick Look, Cover Flow, and searching with Spotlight, see Chapter 3.

Time Machine

If you've been following the Mac OS X Leopard hype, you've no doubt heard lots about Time Machine, which lets you back up your Mac and retrieve files that once might have been lost. Time Machine keeps hourly backups for the last 24 hours, daily backups for the past month, and weekly backups until your backup disk is full. When your backup disk is full, Time Machine drops the oldest backup to free up space for a new one.

WARNING

You shouldn't back up to another partition on an internal drive. If that drive fails, all of your data—and your backup from Time Machine—is lost.

To use Time Machine, first you need to turn it on and configure the settings for where your backups will be stored, and for what you would like to have backed up from your Mac. To do this, click the Time Machine icon in the Dock, or go to System Preferences → Time Machine and move the slider from Off to On, as shown in Figure 1-2.

Figure 1-2. Turn on Time Machine in System Preferences → Time Machine

The next step in the process is to click the Choose Backup Disk button and select an *external* drive that you'll back up your data to, as shown in Figure 1-3.

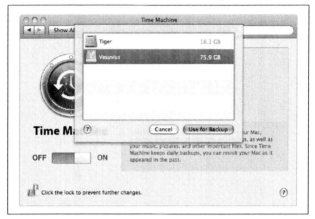

Figure 1-3. Choose an external drive to use as your backup disk

The first backup (shown in Figure 1-4) will take longer than future backups, mainly because Time Machine backs up everything at first, and then only the files that have changed, or have been added or deleted in future backups.

Once the data on your Mac has been backed up to an external or networked drive, you can search for files from previous backups by clicking Time Machine's icon in the Dock. When you click this, your Desktop disappears and you're taken into space as Time Machine comes to the front (shown in Figure 1-5).

If there is a file you want to restore, simply locate the file in one of your backups by clicking on the arrows to the right. Once you've found the file, select it with the mouse and then click Time Machine's Restore button (to the far right along the bottom of the screen), and the file will be restored to that location on your hard drive.

Time Machine makes it really simple for you to back up the data on your Mac. You just let Time Machine run in the background, or whenever you connect your MacBook or

Figure 1-4. The progress bar along the bottom gives you the status of your backup for Time Machine

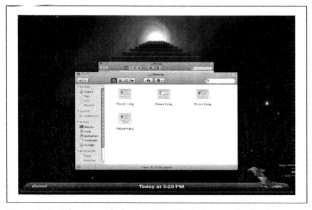

Figure 1-5. When you click Time Machine's icon in the Dock, your Desktop goes away and you're taken back in time (so to speak) so you can recover files

MacBook Pro to an external drive, and it does all the work of backing up your data. And while you hope it never happens, if your hard drive does fail and needs to be replaced, you can restore all of your data to the new drive with the help of Time Machine.

Screen Sharing

How many times have you been on iChat with someone who's having a problem with his Mac, and you're trying to walk him through a fix? Countless, right? And every time you're trying to diagnose the problem, you're pulling your hair out because you're thinking, "Man, if I could just access his system, I'd have this done in seconds!", right? Right. Well, you can send that thank-you note to *sjobs@apple.com*, because Apple has finally built some of Apple Remote Desktop's features into Leopard—and at no extra cost!

When you're in iChat, you'll notice a series of buttons along the bottom of your Buddy List window, as shown in Figure 1-6. The button at the far right, the one that looks like two overlapping displays (similar to the symbols you see on the F7 key) lets you share your computer with the person you're chatting with.

TIP

For this to work, though, you'll both need to be running Mac OS X Leopard. If you select a Buddy's name and the Desktop Sharing button is grayed out and unclickable, that means the person isn't running Leopard on his Mac.

When someone shares his desktop with you, you have total and complete control over his system. When you move the mouse on your end, the mouse moves on his system, which means you can open windows, launch applications, even read his email (but you wouldn't do that, would you?).

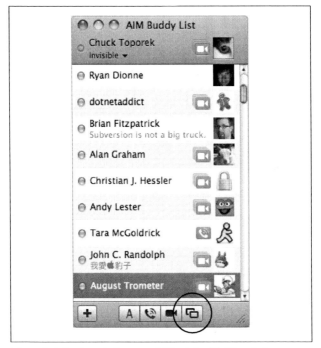

Figure 1-6. Look at the bottom of iChat's Buddy List window to see whether you can share your desktop with one of your friends

Figure 1-7 shows what it looks like when someone else is viewing your desktop. If you look closely, you'll see a smaller window, labeled My Computer, which is a miniature version of your own screen.

To switch back to using your own Mac, click that window and the other user's desktop rotates out of the way so you can get back to work.

For additional control over Screen Sharing, visit the Sharing preference panel (System Preferences → Sharing). You can specify which users on the system, and even friends in your Address Book, you can share your screen with.

Figure 1-7. Screen Sharing lets you take control of someone else's Mac

Quick Look

Quick Look does exactly what its name implies: it lets you quickly take a look inside any file or folder on your Mac.

All you need to do to use Quick Look is select a file and either hit the icon in the Finder's toolbar that looks like an eyeball, or use File → Quick Look (⌘-Y). The file you've selected opens in a preview window above all other windows on the system, as shown in Figure 1-8.

As you can see from Figure 1-8, Quick Look opens this Microsoft Word file in a mini viewer, which lets you scroll through the entire document. If you click on the double arrows along the bottom of the Quick Look window, the file expands into a full-screen view. If you have iPhoto installed on your Mac, any image file you view with Quick Look will have an icon next to the double arrows so you can quickly add the image to your iPhoto Library.

If you use Quick Look on a folder (as shown in Figure 1-9), you won't see the contents of the folder, but instead will see how many files are in the folder, how much space those files take up on your hard drive, and the date and time the contents of that folder were last modified.

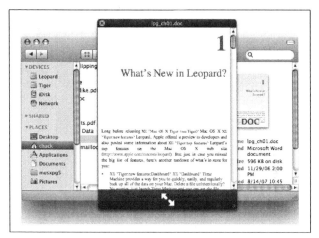

Figure 1-8. Quick Look lets you quickly look inside files and inspect folders

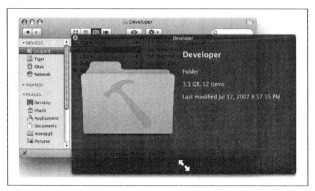

Figure 1-9. Use Quick Look on a folder, and you'll see details about the folder's contents

Quick Look is simple to use (just select a file and hit ⌘-Y), and it makes it super easy for you to quickly examine a file on your Mac.

Spaces

You know how cluttered your screen can get when you have a few applications open at the same time. You have Mail open for email, iCal and Address Book for your appointments and contacts, Word for writing, iChat for staying in contact with your friends, Safari for browsing the Web, and so on. It doesn't take long for your desktop to get cluttered with windows, and even though Exposé is there to help you separate them, you find yourself needing something, well, better. And that's where Spaces comes in.

Spaces takes your Mac's desktop to a new dimension by giving you the option to add additional desktop "spaces" for managing application windows. You configure Spaces in the Exposé & Spaces preference panel (System Preferences → Exposé & Spaces), as shown in Figure 1-10.

By default, Spaces isn't enabled, so if you want to take advantage of it, just turn on the checkbox next to Enable Spaces. Next, use the window in the middle to set the number of rows and columns (you can have up to 16 Spaces on your Mac).

You can also configure Spaces to have a certain application open in a particular Space. As shown in Figure 1-10, my Mac has been configured to have Microsoft Word open in Space 1, iChat and Mail in Space 2, and Safari in Space 4, but you can configure these any way you'd like. Just click the Add button (the one that looks like the plus sign, +), choose the application or utility, choose a Space, and you're all set.

To quickly switch between Spaces, you can use the Control key with the Left or Right Arrow keys on your keyboard, or you can use ⌘-Tab, which brings up the application switcher; select the application you want to use and you're instantly taken to its Space.

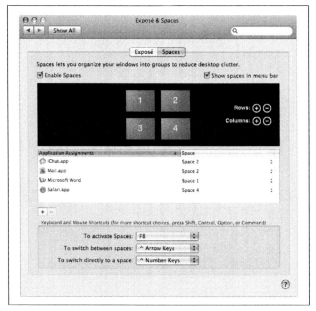

Figure 1-10. Use the Spaces preference panel to configure your Mac's desktop Spaces

To see all of your Spaces, you can either click the Spaces icon in the Dock or hit the F8 key, as shown in Figure 1-11. Once in the Spaces view, you can drag application windows from one Space to another, or click in a Space to quickly go there.

If you're like me, you'll quickly find that Spaces is one of the best new features of Mac OS X Leopard, and it won't take long for you to wonder how you ever lived without it.

Stacks

Stacks offers a new way of viewing and accessing files in folders you store in the Dock. Whenever you download a file from the Internet (such as a PDF file or a disk image), the file is

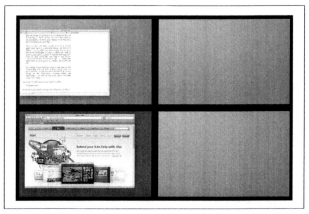

Figure 1-11. Click the Spaces icon in the Dock to see all of your available Spaces and the application windows within

automatically saved to your Downloads folder in your Home directory. What you may not know, however, is that your Downloads folder is also aliased in the Dock, next to the Trash. If you click on the Downloads folder in the Dock, you'll see a list of the files within spring outward (as shown in Figure 1-12) so you can see what's in there.

To open a file in a Stack, simply click its icon and the file opens in the appropriate application. If the item you click on is another folder, that folder opens in a new Finder window. If you don't see what you're looking for, click on the down arrow in the Dock to close the Stack, or click the "Show in Finder" button in the Stack; that closes the Stack and opens a Finder window to that folder.

You're not limited to using just the Downloads folder in the Dock, either. For example, you can open a Finder window and drag your Documents folder to the right side of the Dock as well. This creates an alias of your Documents folder in the Dock, so you can quickly see what's in there.

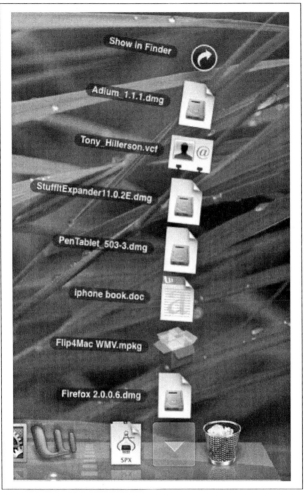

Figure 1-12. Stacks lets you quickly access files in folders you place in the Dock

Improvements to iCal

For the past few versions of Mac OS X, iCal is the one application I've hoped would see improvements, but I have always been left wanting more. Not this time! iCal now has a new interface, as shown in Figure 1-13, and it works more closely with Mail than ever before.

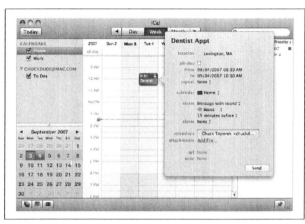

Figure 1-13. iCal finally gets a facelift!

In the new version of iCal, you can:

- Exchange To Do items with Mail
- Add invites to your calendar that you receive in email
- Share your calendar with other Mac users on your local network so they can see when you're available
- Sync your calendar with other devices or computers
- Add a Birthday calendar that pulls birthdates stored in your Address Book
- And much, much more!

The new iCal is a great improvement over its predecessor, so give it a try.

Personalize Messages with Stationery in Mail

Why send an email as plain text when you can spiff it up? When using Mac OS X's Mail application (Applications → Mail), you can opt to send your emails the regular way, or you can click on the Stationery button to add a page design to your email message, as shown in Figure 1-14.

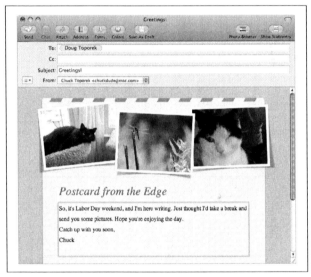

Figure 1-14. Mail's Stationery lets you send messages with style, and with photos from your iPhoto Library

There are more than 20 different Stationery templates you can choose from, just by clicking on the Show Stationery button in a new email message. Want to add your own pictures to the template? Click the Photo Browser button or drag images into the email message from the Finder—it's that simple!

Other Improvements to Mail

In Leopard, Mail is more than just a program for reading and sending emails. Some new features added to Mail in Mac OS X Leopard include:

- The ability to create Notes, for those times when you think of something and want to jot it down as a reminder to yourself.
- Create To Do items, assign them dates and times, and have them show up in iCal, too.
- Use Mail to subscribe to RSS feeds, rather than using Safari.

Parental Controls

It's hard to catch the evening news without hearing another story about some teenager who's been stalked online by a predator. Parents have very few resources at their disposal to help protect their kids from bad things on the Internet…that is, until now.

Mac OS X Leopard sports some powerful Parental Controls, which you can configure using its preference panel in System Preferences (see Figure 1-15).

As you can see from Figure 1-15, the Parental Controls panel has five tabs that allow you to tweak and set controls for your child (or employee). See the section "Parental Controls" in Chapter 2 for more details.

Boot Camp

Boot Camp lets users install and run Windows XP or Windows Vista on their Intel Mac. To use Boot Camp, you'll need an Intel Mac (such as a MacBook, MacBook Pro, Mac Pro, or one of the newer Intel-based iMac or Mac minis).

Figure 1-15. Leopard's Parental Controls give parents the power they need to protect their children

Boot Camp partitions your Mac's hard drive to create a space for you to install Windows on your Mac. Once installed, you can opt to boot into Mac OS X or Windows by setting the default OS in System Preferences → Startup Disk.

TIP

For more details about how to use Boot Camp to install a version of Windows on your Intel Mac, see my digital Short Cut, "Running Boot Camp," available from O'Reilly.

These are just some of the many new features that have been added to Mac OS X Leopard. As you work your way through this book, you'll become aware of even more, but these should give you a taste of what's to come.

CHAPTER 2

Mac OS X Survival Guide

If you're one of the many switchers who've come over to Mac OS X, or even if you've been using Mac OS X since the early public beta (back when Mac OS X was going through its infancy 10.0 and 10.1 phases), this chapter is for you. Here, you'll quickly get up to speed on how to use Mac OS X, from learning about the Finder to learning how to create folders (including the new Smart and Burn folders), to discovering tips, tricks, and keyboard shortcuts to make your Mac life more enjoyable.

Your User Account

When you first install Mac OS X Leopard (or when you boot your new Mac for the first time), you have to create at least one user for the system. You'll be asked to assign a name, short name, and password, as well as provide address information for the user. You'll also set up some very basic preferences, such as the date and time zone, and configure basic network settings.

By default, the first user you set up on your Mac is known as an "administrative user," which means that user can pretty much do whatever he wants with the system, including setting up or removing user accounts. As an admin user, you can create accounts for other users (such as your wife and kids) on your system, manage their settings, and also delete their accounts when necessary.

After you create the admin user account, Mac OS X logs into that account, and then you're off and running. And every time you boot your Mac, the system automatically logs into this account unless you add another user account or change the settings in the Accounts preference panel (System Preferences → Accounts).

What's in Your Home Folder?

Regardless of how many users are on your system, every user's Home folder is really a subfolder within the Users folder. For example, if you have two users on your system whose short names (which are assigned when you create user accounts) are *chuck* and *bob*, their Home folders show up in the Finder by navigating to Macintosh HD → Users → *username* (in this case, either *chuck* or *bob*).

Every user on a Mac OS X system has a default set of folders, found within her own Home folder. These folders can be used for storing anything you desire, although some have specific purposes, as noted here:

Desktop
> While you might think of your desktop as that thing that sits beneath all the windows on your Mac, it is actually a folder in itself. The Desktop folder contains the items found on your desktop, including any files, folders, or application aliases you've placed there.

Is Automatic Login Secure?

The short answer to that is *no*. If your Mac is set up to auto-matically log on to your user account, all somebody needs to do is boot your machine and he has easy access to all your information. While you might not think this is such an issue if you're using your Mac at home, think again. If someone breaks into your house or apartment and steals your beloved Mac, the thief not only has your computer, but automatic login gives him free reign over all your info.

If you're security conscious and you don't want the system to automatically log in to your account (or that of another user) at startup, you can disable this setting by going to the Accounts panel, clicking Login Options, and turning off the checkbox next to "Automatically log in as."

Right above that, you'll see options for how the Login Win-dow appears at startup. You can set this so the Login Window displays a list of users or requires users to enter both their user-name and password. With the "List of users" option, the Login Window displays a list of users for the system, along with any graphical icon they've set for their user account. To log in, simply click on the appropriate username (the others then disappear), enter the password in the space provided, and then either hit Return or click the Log In button.

Of the two options, "List of users" is probably the least secure, because all someone needs to do is guess your password. By requiring users to enter *both* their username and password, you ensure that they actually know the short username for the user account. Just because my name is Chuck Toporek doesn't necessarily mean that's the name I use for my account (as defined in the Short Name field of the Accounts panel).

And if you're really paranoid (like me), you should enable File-Vault protection for your user account, using the Security preference panel (System Preferences → Security). For more information about the Security panel and FileVault, see the "Security" section, later in this chapter.

Documents

> While it isn't mandatory, the Documents folder can be used as a repository for any files or folders you create. Most applications, such as TextEdit, Microsoft Word, and the new iWork's Pages application, save files here by default.

Downloads

> New for Mac OS X Leopard is the Downloads folder. Whenever you download a file or image from the Internet, those files are automatically saved to the Downloads folder. There's also a Stack for the Downloads folder in the Dock, just to the left of the Trash. If you click on that icon, icons for the items in the Downloads folder fan out (as shown earlier in Figure 1-12) to give you quick and easy access to the files within.

Library

> This folder contains preference files, known in Mac OS X land as *property lists files*, or *plist* files (so-named because of their *.plist* file extension). These plist files are used by applications to store the preferences you set.

Movies

>This is a place where you can store movies you create with iMovie, DVD projects you create with iDVD, or Quick-Time movies you create or download from the Internet.

Music

>This directory is used to store music and sound files, including *.aiff*, *.mp3*, and others. This is also where your iTunes Library, and the music you purchase through the iTunes Music Store, are located.

Pictures

>This directory can be used as a place to store photos and other images. iPhoto also uses the Pictures directory to store your iPhoto Library.

TIP

iMovie, iDVD, iPhoto, GarageBand, and iWeb are bundled and sold together as iLife '08 (available from *http://www.apple.com/ilife*). iTunes remains a free download from Apple's web site (*http://www.apple.com/itunes*) and is included as part of Mac OS X Leopard's base of installed applications.

Public

>If you enable File or Web Sharing (System Preferences → Services), this is where you place items you want to share with other users on your system. Users who access your Public folder can see and copy items from this directory.

>Also located within the Public folder is the Drop Box folder. If you enable File Sharing (System Preferences → Services → File Sharing), this is where other users can place files after connecting to your Mac.

Sites

>If you enable Web Sharing (System Preferences → Services → Web Sharing), this folder will contain the web site for your user account.

If your system has more than one user on it, you'll find a Shared folder within the Users folder. Because users are allowed to add or modify files only within their own Home folder, the Shared folder is a place where you can place items to be shared with other users on the same system.

Logging In and Fast User Switching

If you have more than one user on your system, you can enable Fast User Switching in the Accounts preference panel (System Preferences → Accounts). In the left column of the Accounts panel, click the Login Options button at the very bottom. This switches the panel's view to the right, which allows you to enable and configure the settings for how users log in to your system.

By default, Mac OS X has the "Automatically log in as" option checked, and you should see your username in the pop-up menu next to this item. If you have more than one user on your Mac, and you're not sure who will log in when, you should uncheck this option.

Sleep Mode, Logging Out, and Shutting Down

When you've reached the end of your day, you've got three options for dealing with your Mac. You can:

- Log out of your account (Shift-⌘-Q), which takes you out of your user environment, placing you at a login screen where you'll need to enter your username and password to gain access to the system again.

- Shut down the system by selecting → Shut Down. Selecting this option logs you out of your user account and powers off your Mac.

- Put your Mac to sleep by selecting → Sleep. If you have a MacBook or MacBook Pro, you can just close the display (or "lid") of your laptop, and your Mac automatically goes into Sleep mode.

Do you need to shut down at the end of every day? No, not really. Depending on how you've configured the Energy Saver preferences (System Preferences → Energy Saver), you can just put your Mac to sleep every night, or let it fall asleep based on the preference settings you've made, and everything should be OK.

TIP

It's very common for Mac users to reboot (or restart) Mac OS X only when there is a critical Software Update that forces you to restart, such as a Security Update or an upgrade to a newer version of Mac OS X.

The advantage to putting your Mac into Sleep mode is that it keeps the system running so you don't have to wait for your Mac to start up again (not that it takes very long for Mac OS X to boot anyway). In Sleep mode, your Mac uses a very minimal amount of energy to keep the system running, which saves you (or your company) money in the long run. To wake up your Mac from Sleep mode, just hit the Return key on your keyboard. The hard drive spins up, and your Mac jumps back to life, ready for you to go to work.

Startup and Shutdown Keys

For most users, starting and shutting down your Mac is fairly routine: press the Power-On button to start, and go to → Shut Down to turn your Mac off at night. But there are times when you need to do more, for whatever reason. Table 2-1 lists some of the additional keys you can use when starting, restarting, logging out, and shutting down your system.

NOTE

Some of the keyboard shortcuts listed in Table 2-1 only work on newer hardware. If you are using an older Mac, these keyboard shortcuts might not work.

Table 2-1. Keyboard shortcuts used for starting, restarting, logging out, and shutting down

Key command	Description
C	Holding down the C key at startup boots from a CD or DVD (useful when installing or upgrading the system software).
N	Attempts to start up from a NetBoot server.
R	Resets the display for a Mac laptop (PowerBook, iBook, MacBook, or MacBook Pro).
T	Holding down the T key at startup places your Mac into Target mode as a mountable FireWire drive. After starting up, your screen will have a blue background with a floating yellow FireWire symbol. Target mode makes the hard drive(s) of your Mac appear as mounted FireWire drive(s) when connected to another system. To exit Target mode, press the Power-On button to turn off your Mac. After your Mac has shut down completely, press the Power-On button again to restart your Mac.
X	Holding down the X key at startup forces your Mac to boot into Mac OS X, even if Mac OS 9 is specified as the default startup disk.
⌘-S	Boots into single-user mode (something you'll only need to do when troubleshooting your system, or if you're a system administrator).
⌘-V	Boots into verbose mode, displaying all the startup messages onscreen. (Linux users will be familiar with this.)
Shift	Holding down the Shift key at startup invokes Safe Boot mode, turning off any unnecessary kernel extensions (kexts) and ignoring anything you've set in the Accounts preferences panel.
Option	Holding down the Option key at startup opens the Startup Manager, which allows you to select which OS to boot into. Keep this in mind if you've installed Windows XP or Vista on your Intel Mac with Boot Camp.
Mouse button	Holding down the mouse button at startup ejects any disk (CD, DVD, or other removable media) that might still be in the drive.

Table 2-1. Keyboard shortcuts used for starting, restarting, logging out, and shutting down (continued)

Key command	Description
Shift-Option-⌘-Q Option + 🍎 → Log Out Option-Power-On	Logs you off without first prompting you.
Option + 🍎 → Shut Down	Shuts down your system without first prompting you.
Option + 🍎 → Restart	Restarts your machine without first prompting you.
Control-⌘-Power-On	Forces an automatic shutdown of your system; this should be used only as a last resort because it could mess up your filesystem.[a]
Control-Eject	Opens a dialog box that contains options for Restart, Sleep, and Shutdown.
Control-Option-⌘-Eject	Quits all applications and shuts the system down. If there are any application windows open with unsaved changes, you will be prompted to save the changes before the application is forced to quit.

[a] Mostly, you'll just wait at the gray Apple startup screen while a Unix command (*fsck*, short for *filesystem check*) runs in the background, cleaning up any goobers on your system.

Quick Tips for Users

Here are some helpful hints for managing your user account:

Configure my login?
> System Preferences → Accounts → *username* → Login Options.

Change my login password?
> System Preferences → Accounts → *username* → Password.

TIP

When choosing a password, you should avoid using dictionary words (i.e., common, everyday words found in the dictionary) or something that could be easily guessed. To improve your security, choose an alphanumeric password. Remember, passwords are case-sensitive, so you can mix upper- and lowercase letters in your password as well.

Add another user to the system?

System Preferences → Accounts → click on the Add button (+) below the Login Options button (requires administrator privileges).

TIP

Unix administrators might be tempted to use the *useradd*, *userdel*, and *usermod* commands to add, remove, and modify a user, respectively, from the Terminal. The only problem is, you can't—these commands don't exist on Mac OS X.

Remove a user from the system?

System Preferences → Accounts → *username* → click on the minus sign (–) below the Login Options button (requires administrator privileges). After a user has been deleted, that user's directories (and everything within) are packaged up in a disk image (as *username.dmg*) and placed in the */Users/Deleted Users* folder. Only a user with administrator privileges can delete this disk image.

NOTE

Obviously, you can't remove your own user account when you're logged in to the system. If you want to remove your user account from the system, you have to log out and log back in as another user.

Give a user administrator privileges?

System Preferences → Accounts → *username* → Password → turn on the checkbox next to "Allow user to administer this computer" (requires administrator privileges).

Restrict which applications a user can use?

System Preferences → Parental Controls → *username* → System → turn on the checkbox next to "Only allow selected applications," and then choose which applications to allow the user to use from the list of applications. Parental Controls are discussed in the "Parental Controls" section, next.

Keep a user from changing her password?

System Preferences → Parental Controls → *username* → System → turn off the "Can change password" option.

Turn off automatic login?

System Preferences → Security → General → enable the checkbox next to "Disable automatic login."

Turn on Fast User Switching?

System Preferences → Accounts → *username* → Login Options → click on the checkbox next to "Enable fast user switching."

Set a password hint?

System Preferences → Accounts → *username* → Password → Change Password. When you click the Change Password button, a sheet slides down from the title bar, asking you to provide your current password. Enter your password and then tab down to the Password Hint field; just enter some text in this field that will help you remember your password (such as "Who's your daddy?") and hit Return to save the change.

Find out which users have admin privileges?

System Preferences → Accounts. Users with administrator privileges have the word "Admin" beneath their name in the list of users in the left column. Unrestricted users will have the word "Standard" beneath their username, and users who have Parental Controls enabled on their account will have the word "Managed" beneath their username.

Parental Controls

Apple introduced an entirely new set of Parental Controls in Mac OS X Leopard, which you can apply to nonadministrator user accounts on your Mac. To turn on and configure Parental Controls, open System Preferences and click the icon for the Parental Controls preference panel. When the panel opens (as shown in Figure 2-1), you will see a list of users on the left to which you can apply Parental Controls.

Figure 2-1. Before you can Enable Parental Controls, you must first authenticate as an administrative user by clicking the Lock icon, circled at the lower-left corner

---

TIP

You cannot apply Parental Controls to a user when she is logged in to the system. To see which users are currently logged in to the system, click the user menu (next to the Spotlight menu in the menu bar). Users who are logged in to the system will have an orange checkmark next to their name.

Before you can apply Parental Controls on another user, you must first authenticate yourself as an administrative user on the system. To do this, click the Lock icon in the lower-left corner (circled in Figure 2-1) and enter your password in the dialog box that appears. Now select a user in the left panel and click the Enable Parental Controls button.

As shown in Figure 2-2, the Parental Controls window has five tabs (System, Content, Mail & iChat, Time Limits, and Logs), which are described as follows.

Figure 2-2. The Parental Controls preference panel lets you restrict which applications a user can use

System

The options in the System tab allow you to control the things the user can do on the system. For example, you can restrict the user's access to certain applications, force him to use the Simple Finder, prevent him from modifying the Dock, or even keep him from burning CDs or DVDs.

The Simple Finder provides a very, well, simple view of the system. The user's Dock contains only the Finder icon (which does nothing when you click on it), an Applications folder that lists icons for the applications a user is permitted to use, a Documents folder, access to the Shared folder for sharing documents with other users, and the Trash. The user won't be able to change the Dock, and he cannot create new folders; his wings are pretty well clipped.

Content

This tab has two sections, the first of which lets you hide profane words in the Dictionary application, while the second lets you determine which web sites the user may visit. When it comes to controlling web access, you have three options to choose from:

Allow unrestricted access to websites

With this option selected, the user will have unfettered access to any web site on the Internet.

Try to limit access to adult websites automatically

With this option selected, the user will have access to most web sites on the Internet, with the exception of sites known to contain pornography. The key word in this option is "Try," in that the Parental Controls bases this restriction on known adult web sites. You can configure this option further by clicking the Configure button and adding URLs for web sites you catch the person using.

Allow access to only these websites

The final option permits access only to a limited set of web sites, mostly ones that your child would only want access to. The sites permitted in this list include:

- Discovery Kids
- PBS Kids
- HowStuffWorks
- National Geographic – Kids
- Yahoo! Kids
- Disney
- Scholastic.com

- Smithsonian Institution
- Time for Kids

You can add and remove sites to that list by clicking the Add (+) button, or by selecting one of the sites in the list and clicking the Remove (–) button.

Mail & iChat

Here you can specify which people your child (or employee) is permitted to communicate with over email and instant messaging (IM) with iChat. And what if your child tries to contact someone who isn't in the safe list? You can specify an email address for permission requests to be sent so you can authorize email and messaging to someone who hasn't been preapproved.

You can also restrict which addresses this user can send email to. This feature (which is turned on by default) first sends the email to another person (presumably the parent or system administrator), who can grant permission for the email to be sent to the original address. This lets you specify a preapproved list of people with whom the user is allowed to chat over iChat.

Time Limits

For parents who worry about how much time their children spend on the computer, this tab is a lifesaver. Here you can specify how much time your children are allowed access to the Internet for weekdays or weekend days, and you can even prevent them from using the computer before or after certain hours.

Logs

While it might seem a bit "Big Brother"-ish, this tab lets you see which web sites were visited and blocked, which applications were used and when, and with whom your child was IMing on iChat.

Parental Controls gives you as an administrator a lot of power and control over what a user can do on the system.

Using Software Update

From time to time, Apple releases patches to Mac OS X and its other applications, such as the iLife apps, and, on occasion, security patches to block holes that could put your Mac (and the data on it) at risk. To keep your system up-to-date, Apple provides a Software Update application (accessible either through the System Preferences → Software Update preference panel, or via → Software Update).

TIP

Whenever you install a new version of Mac OS X, or any Apple application for that matter, it's always wise to run Software Update to see if there's a new patch for your system.

Software Update's preference panel, shown in Figure 2-3, gives you the option of checking for updates Daily, Weekly, or Monthly. When you click Check Now, Software Update records the day and time that you checked for updates, and uses this information as the basis for when to check for the next update. For example, if you have Software Update set to look for updates Daily (through the "Check for updates" pop-up menu), and the last time you checked for an update was yesterday at 6:21 p.m., it automatically checks for updates at *that* time every day.

You also have the option to have Software Update automatically "Download important updates in the background" by turning on this checkbox. With this option enabled, Software Update checks for updates on its regularly scheduled basis, and if it finds something critical you need (such as a Security Update that protects your Mac), it automatically downloads that item to your system. Once the item has downloaded, a dialog box appears, giving you the option to install the update at your leisure.

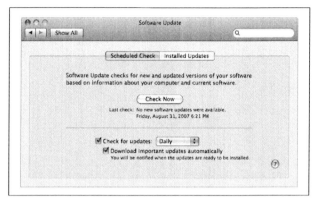

Figure 2-3. Use the Software Update panel to keep your system (and any Apple applications you're running) up-to-date

Saving Your Updates

If you manage more than one Mac system (for example, your Mac Pro, your wife's MacBook, and your kids' iMac), running Software Update on all the machines not only takes each person a lot of time, but also taps out your bandwidth. One solution to this problem is to download the updates from Apple's Mac OS X software page, found online at *http://www.apple.com/downloads/macosx*.

You'll not only find the latest updates and software patches there, but you'll also find Combo Updates for Mac OS X, each of which are downloadable as disk images that can be burned to CD or DVD. Once you've burned those disk images, you can take that CD or DVD to each machine and install the update by mounting the disk image and double-clicking the installer.

Mac OS X's Combo Updates come in particularly handy when you need to do a clean install on a system. For example, say that Apple releases an update to Mac OS X Leopard, putting it at version 10.5.3, but you decide that it's time to do a clean install, reformat your hard drive, and maybe partition your hard drive. When you gut your system like that, you'll need to do a fresh install of Leopard, which means you're back to version 10.5. And while you *could* run Software Update and install all the updates from there, if you've burned the latest Combo Update to CD, you can just pop in that disc and double-click the installer, making the update process go faster since you're not downloading a bunch of system updates.

Security

Mac OS X Leopard offers some powerful built-in security features that every user should take advantage of. Regardless of whether your Mac is at work or home, or if you never, ever go online, there are some basic things you should consider setting up on your Mac to protect your user account and your precious data.

FileVault

Introduced with Mac OS X Panther (version 10.3), FileVault allows you to encrypt and protect everything within your Home folder. FileVault uses a 128-bit data encryption scheme, which means it's very hard to crack. To enable File-Vault for your user account, go to the FileVault tab in the Security preferences panel and click the Turn On FileVault button. FileVault uses your login password as the passkey to secure the data in your Home folder. While you're at it, you should also click the Set Master Password button to set a master password that allows you to unlock any FileVault account on your computer.

WARNING

If you're going to use FileVault, you should *definitely* set the Master Password for your system. If you or one of the users on the system forgets their FileVault password and the Master Password hasn't been set, all of that user's information is lost (unless you want to pay a security expert thousands of dollars to crack the encryption).

The one caveat to using FileVault is that if you forget your password and you haven't set the Master Password (or if you forget both passwords), there is absolutely no way to decrypt your FileVault-protected Home folder. If you can't remember either password, all of your data is lost. If you are going to use FileVault, you should write these passwords down and hide them from plain sight (or in your bank's safety deposit box, if you have one). That way, if you ever do forget your passwords, you'll at least (hopefully) remember where you wrote them down so you can retrieve your data.

Keychains

Just like the keys you carry in your pocket to unlock your house or start your car, the Mac OS X Keychain service helps you manage and keep track of all the usernames and passwords you have—for everything from your user account to the information you provide to log on to your favorite web site or network file server. Keychains have been around since Mac OS 9 and have continued to improve along with Mac OS X.

Every user has a Keychain file, which is stored in your Home → Library → Keychains folder. The Keychain file is encrypted and can only be viewed with the aid of the Keychain Access program (*/Applications/Utilities*). You can use this program to add or delete items in your Keychain, create and store an encrypted note, and more. You can also search for specific items in your Keychain, which comes in handy when you've forgotten the password to your AIM account, for example. This is a great improvement because, in the past, you'd have to sift through the items in your Keychain and hope to find the item you were looking for. Now, all you need to do is type a few letters in the Search field, and you can quickly find it.

Keep Keychain Access in mind when you've forgotten a password to something. Chances are, if you've had to authenticate yourself to a web site, the information you need is stored in your Keychain.

WARNING

Because your Keychain contains all of your passwords (and maybe that encrypted note, ranting about your boss), you should consider backing up your Keychain regularly. There are many ways to do this, such as backing it up to your iDisk (if you have a .Mac account) or dragging the Home → Library → Keychains folder to an external drive.

If you're feeling a little less secure about these ideas, you might consider using Disk Utility (*/Applications/Utilities*) to create an encrypted and password-protected disk image of your Keychains folder.

Firewall Settings

If you're taking your Mac online—regardless of whether you're at home or at work—you really should enable Mac OS X's built-in firewall. Basically, a firewall protects your Mac from unwanted intrusions from people trying to pry into your Mac and steal your data while you're online. Even though Macs are more secure than most Windows PCs, you're still prone to attacks, especially if you use a broadband connection to the Internet, such as DSL or a cable modem.

Leopard's firewall is on by default, and there are two ways to manage its settings. The first is in the Sharing preference panel (System Preferences → Sharing). When you open the Sharing preferences, you'll notice that there's a list of Services off to the left. These Services are things that can make your Mac vulnerable to attack, so they're turned off by default. To turn on a Service, simply click the checkbox. For example, if you want to enable File Sharing, click the checkbox next to the Service, and then use the right side of the window to configure what sort of access people (users and outsiders) will have to files on your Mac, as shown in Figure 2-4.

Figure 2-4. Use the menus in the far right column of the Sharing pane to restrict access to shared services

This is a little more work than it was in the past with earlier versions of Mac OS X, but trust me, this provides you with a greater level of security, since you can tweak the settings by user rather than for the entire service. If you look closely at Figure 2-4, you'll notice that there is an Options button there as well. When you click this, a sheet slides down with options for you to share files and folders via FTP or SMB.

TIP

The options available on the right side of the Sharing Panel are different for each Service. For example, the Screen Sharing service lets you select who you can share your screen with, including users on the system or people in your Address Book. Take the time to look over the options for each service and set them according to your own comfort levels.

The second way you can tweak your firewall settings is in the Firewall tab of the Security preference panel (System Preferences → Security → Firewall). In comparison to the Sharing preference panel, the Firewall pane looks a little sparse. Here you have only three additional options to choose from:

Allow all incoming connections
> This allows all incoming connections to the applications and services on your Mac. For example, this permits others to log in to your Mac remotely for things like file, screen, and web sharing.

Block all incoming connections
> This blocks all incoming traffic and remote or local connections to your Mac. This is probably the strongest setting you can choose for your firewall.

Limit incoming connections to specific services and applications
> This option lets you pick and choose which applications (and their applicable services) can have access to the outside world. For example, if you want to allow access for iChat, click the Add (+) button, and then select iChat from the sheet that slides down. You can further tweak its settings by using the up and down arrows to the right to choose the limit for each item (either "Allow all incoming connections," or "Block all incoming connections").

If you select either "Block all incoming connections" or "Limit incoming connections…", you'll notice that the Advanced button becomes available. When this button is clicked, you're presented with two additional firewall options:

Enable Firewall Logging
> This turns on firewall logging and provides you with details about any attempts some punk might have made to break through your firewall. Click Open Log to view the logfile (*/var/log/appfirewall.log*) in the Console application.

Enable Stealth Mode

> With Stealth Mode turned on, if anyone attempts to gain access to your computer, he won't even get a response that your computer exists. Think of this as an invisibility cloak for your computer; you can go on the network/ Internet, and anyone that tries to access your computer illegally from the opposite end won't even see your computer there.

Apple wouldn't have provided these features without good reason, so if you want to protect yourself—and your computer—you should consider turning on both of these options.

Sharing Services

As noted in the Firewall section, the Sharing preference panel lets you configure how your Mac shares data and services with other users. By default, all of the services listed in this pane are unchecked; to enable a service, just click the checkbox and continue tweaking its settings to the right. The options provided here include:

Screen Sharing

> This allows you to share your screen with others who are using Mac OS X Leopard. When you share your screen with another user, she has control of your mouse, can start and quit applications, etc. Keep this option in mind for times when you need help with something, or when you need to help someone else sort out a problem on her Mac.

File Sharing

> Allows users of other computers to access your Public folder, located within your Home folder.

Printer Sharing

> Allows you to share print services with other Mac computers on your network.

Web Sharing

When enabled, allows people to view any web pages you've saved in your Sites folder.

Remote Login

Allows you to log on to your Mac remotely, using the Secure Shell (SSH) from a Unix shell program.

Remote Management

Allows others to access your computer using Apple Remote Desktop (*http://www.apple.com/remotedesktop*). If someone is using ARD, he can view everything you're doing on your computer, and he can also take control of your Mac.

TIP

Most Mac users won't use ARD; however, in larger corporate environments it's fairly common for system administrators to use it to help users get out of a mess or to install applications and software updates.

Remote Apple Events

Allows applications on other Macs to send remote Apple Events to your computer. Apple Events are little messages a program can send via AppleScript to your computer or to any application on your computer.

Xgrid

When enabled, an Xgrid controller can add your Mac as a distributed computing node to harness your Mac's available processing power. Most home users won't have to worry about enabling this service, but if you're in a work environment—particularly if you're surrounded by scientists, engineers, and software developers who are also using Mac OS X Leopard—you'd be wise to leave this option turned off; otherwise, you might notice your Mac slowing down when you least expect it.

Internet Sharing
> Allows you to share your Internet connection with other computers.

Bluetooth Sharing
> This allows you to share files with other Bluetooth-enabled computers and devices.

These items are disabled by default, mainly because enabling them opens up a network port to your computer, allowing other computer users to gain access to your Mac. Enable these services judiciously. For example, you might want to turn on File Sharing only when you need to share files with another user. Then, as soon as you've swapped files, don't forget to turn it off.

Remember, the fewer network ports you have open to your Mac, the less likely you are to have some intruder gain access and wreak havoc on your system.

Other Security Features

Some other things you can do to protect your Mac against possible intruders include turning on the following options found in the Security preference panel (System Preferences → Security → General):

Require password to wake this computer from sleep or screen saver
> This way you can enable the screensaver or put your Mac to sleep (→ Sleep) when you know you're going to be away from your Mac, even for a small amount of time. If someone tries to use your computer or wake it from sleep, she'll be prompted to give your password, and if she doesn't know it, she won't be able to gain access to your Mac.

Disable automatic login
> Remember, by disabling automatic login, you force users to authenticate with their username and password at login.

Require password to unlock each secure system preference

By enabling this option, you force users to authenticate with a valid password before they can use any of the following preference panels: Security, Energy Saver, Print & Fax, Network, Sharing, Accounts, Date & Time, Parental Controls, and Startup Disk. This keeps unwanted users from doing malicious things, such as creating or deleting user accounts or disabling your screensaver, to name a couple. Anyone who tries to access these preference panels will see a locked padlock icon in the lower-left corner. To use that panel, you need to click the padlock and authenticate with the current user's password.

Log out after XX minutes of inactivity

With this option you can specify a number of minutes your Mac must be inactive for the system to automatically log you out of your account. By default, this option is set to 60 minutes, but you can change it to anything from 1 minute up to 960 minutes (16 hours).

Use secure virtual memory

This option prevents others from being able to read any virtual memory data left on your hard drive. After enabling this feature, you must restart your Mac for this to work.

Disable remote control infrared receiver

This disables the IR remote sensor in newer Mac models, such as the MacBook, MacBook Pro, and iMacs that come with an IR remote for use with Front Row. You can also pair your Mac's IR remote by clicking the Pair button and then holding down the Menu and Next buttons on the remote. Hold the remote buttons down until the pairing graphics appear on screen, as shown in Figure 2-5.

Just remember that if someone really wants to get at the data on your Mac, there's a way around every security feature (crackers are pretty smart, you know). However, enabling these options should help you safeguard your Mac against most intrusions.

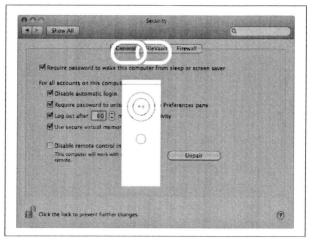

Figure 2-5. This is what you will see onscreen when you've successfully paired your Mac's infrared remote with your computer

Password Security

Finally, one of the last things you can do to protect your data is to use a secure password for your user account. When choosing a password, try not to use a common word that can be found in any dictionary. You should try to use a password that's an alphanumeric series of characters, using a combination of numbers and upper- and lowercase letters; for example, *x41Lm89z* (or something along those lines).

To help you choose a secure password, Leopard offers a Password Assistant (System Preferences → Accounts → *username* → Change Password → click the key icon next to New Password), which you can use to test the strength of your existing password. If it's weak, you can use the Password Assistant to help you find one that's more secure.

Force Quitting Applications

Every now and then, it's bound to happen: you're going to be faced with what's known in Mac circles as the "spinning beach ball of death." You know, that little colored disc that spins around in circles whenever you launch an application? Well, if you're familiar with that, someday, somehow, you'll see it "hang," and just keep on spinning. When that happens, there are a variety of things that could be going on, but it usually just means that an application got stuck doing whatever it was you wanted it to. And when an application is stuck, and you're faced with the spinning beach ball of death, you're going to need to know how to force that application to quit so you can try all over again.

Fortunately, Mac OS X has something known as *protected memory*, which means that every application—including the actual system software—runs in its own protected space. When an application hangs, it typically won't affect the system or any other apps you're running. This is a good thing, and you have the engineers at Apple to thank for it.

There are a few ways to force quit an application, but the easiest way (especially if you aren't a Unix geek) is to use Mac OS X's Force Quit Applications window, which you open by either selecting → Force Quit or using its keyboard shortcut, Option-⌘-Esc. Once this window opens, all you need to do is select the application that's giving you grief and then click the Force Quit button.

Relaunching the Finder

If the Finder seems to hang on you (this can sometimes happen when trying to use the Finder to connect to an FTP site), you'll need to *relaunch* the Finder.

Since the mouse pointer has been replaced with the spinning beach ball of death, chances are you won't be able to click the Apple menu (), so just use the Option-⌘-Esc shortcut to open the Force Quit Applications window. Select the Finder in the list and click the Relaunch button. There is a short pause as the system takes the Finder out of commission temporarily, and you'll see the Dock disappear momentarily. When the Dock pops back into place, that's your cue that the Finder has relaunched successfully and is safe to use once more.

Keyboard Shortcuts

On the Mac (as with Windows) you have two ways of invoking commands in the GUI: by using the menus or by issuing shortcuts for the commands on the keyboard. Not every menu item has a keyboard accelerator, but for the ones that do (the more common functions), using the keyboard shortcuts can save you a lot of time.

Basic Keyboard Shortcuts

Table 2-2 lists the common key commands found in Mac OS X. While most of these commands function the same way across all applications, some—such as ⌘-B and ⌘-I—can vary among programs, and others might work only when the Finder is active. For example, ⌘-B in Microsoft Word turns on boldface type or makes a selection bold, but in Xcode, ⌘-B builds your application. Likewise, ⌘-I in Word italicizes a word or selection, but hitting ⌘-I after selecting a file, folder, or application on the Desktop or in the Finder opens the Show Info window for the selected item.

Table 2-2. Common keyboard shortcuts

Key command	Task
Option-⌘-Escape	Open the Force Quit window.
⌘-Tab ⌘-Tab, Right Arrow	Cycle forward through active applications.
Shift-⌘-Tab ⌘-Tab, Left Arrow	Cycle backward through active applications.
⌘-Space	Search with Spotlight.
⌘-`	Cycle through an application's open windows.

Table 2-2. Common keyboard shortcuts (continued)

Key command	Task
⌘-.	Cancel operation.
⌘-?	Open Mac Help.
⌘-[	Go back in the Finder view to the previous item.
⌘-]	Go forward in the Finder view to the previous item.
⌘-Up Arrow	Go to the folder that contains a selected item.
Shift-⌘-G	Go to a specific folder in the Finder.
⌘-A	Select all.
Option-⌘-T	Hide/reveal the Finder's toolbar.
⌘-C	Copy.
⌘-D	Duplicate; creates a duplicate copy of a selected item. This command adds the word "copy" to the filename before the file extension. For example, if you were to select the file *file.txt* and hit ⌘-D, a new file named *copy.txt* (with a space in the filename) is created in the same directory as *file.txt*).
⌘-L	Create an alias of a file.
Option-⌘-D	Turn Dock hiding on/off.
⌘-Delete	Move item to Trash.
Shift-⌘-Delete	Empty Trash.
⌘-E	Eject the selected disk image, CD, etc.
F8	If you have Spaces turned on, this changes your display to show all of your Spaces and the application windows open within each space.
⌘-F	Find.
⌘-H	Hide application.
⌘-I	Get Info.
⌘-J	Show View options in the Finder.
⌘-K	Connect to Server.
Shift-⌘-K	Connect to a specific network.

Table 2-2. Common keyboard shortcuts (continued)

Key command	Task
⌘-M	Minimize window.
Option-⌘-M	Minimize all open windows for an application.
⌘-N	Open a new Finder window (this is a change from earlier versions of the Mac OS, where ⌘-N was used to create new folders).
Shift-⌘-N	Create new folder.
Option-⌘-N	Create new Smart Folder.
⌘-O	Open file or folder; can also be used to launch applications.
⌘-P	Print file.
⌘-Q	Quit application.
⌘-R	Show original.
⌘-T	Add an item to the Finder's Sidebar.
Option-⌘-T	Hide the Finder's Toolbar.
⌘-V	Paste.
⌘-W	Close window.
Option-⌘-W	Close all open windows for an application.
⌘-X	Cut.
⌘-Y	Quick Look.
⌘-Z	Undo.
Shift-⌘-Z	Redo (not available in all applications).
Shift-⌘-A	Go to the Applications folder in the Finder.
Shift-⌘-U	Go to the Utilities folder in the Finder.
Shift-⌘-C	Go to Computer View in the Finder.
Shift-⌘-H	Go to Home View in the Finder.
Shift-⌘-I	Go to iDisk View in the Finder (requires a .Mac account).
Shift-⌘-3	Take a screenshot of the entire display.
Shift-⌘-4	Make and capture a rectangular selection of the display.

Ten Essential Keyboard Shortcuts

Out of Table 2-2's huge list of keyboard shortcuts, there are 10 that you'll use most often:

1. ⌘-Q to quit an application
2. ⌘-O to open a file while you're in an application
3. ⌘-P to print documents
4. ⌘-W to close windows
5. ⌘-C to copy something you've selected in a file to the Clipboard
6. ⌘-V to paste something you've copied to the Clipboard to another location
7. ⌘-X to cut something you've selected out of a file and move it to the Clipboard
8. ⌘-A to select everything in a file or folder (or all of the items on your desktop)
9. ⌘-S to save a file (something you should do often)
10. ⌘-Z to undo something you shouldn't have done

You'll quickly notice patterns when you use these shortcuts. For example, you'll find that ⌘-C and ⌘-V go hand in hand, as you'll often copy something first and then quickly paste it into another file, email, Sticky Note, etc. The difference between Copy (⌘-C) and Cut (⌘-X) is that the item you've copied stays put, whereas something you cut disappears. Keep this in mind as you master the fine art of moving stuff around in and between files.

And keep ⌘-Z in your back pocket for those times when you need to undo something. For example, say you've just finished writing your master's thesis and you decide you want to change the font. You quickly hit ⌘-A to select all of the text in the document, and then accidentally hit the Delete key. Poof! Everything is gone in the blink of an eye. But all hope is not lost. Just hit that faithful ⌘-Z key and your text is right back where you want it. Now hit the ⌘-S shortcut to save the file before you try that again.

Once you get the hang of using keyboard shortcuts, you'll find yourself using the menu bar less and less.

CHAPTER 3

Mac OS X Basics

This part of the book introduces you to the key features of Mac OS X's interface. Here we'll cover:

- The menu bar
- The Dock
- Window controls
- The Finder
- Creating new folders
- The Services menu
- Exposé
- The Dashboard
- Spotlight
- Get Info and file permissions

The Menu Bar

Regardless of which application you're using, Mac OS X's menu bar is always located across the top of the screen, yet for Leopard, it takes on a new look and feel. If you take a closer look, you'll notice that the menu bar is transparent and that the Desktop image shows through. You'll also notice that all of the icons are devoid of color—only black or grayscale here—with the exception of the Input menu, if you've turned that on in the International preference panel (System Preferences → International → Input Menu).

There are some standard items you'll always find in the menu bar, but as you switch from application to application, you'll notice that the menu names and some of their options change according to which application is active. Figure 3-1 shows the menu bar as it appears when the Finder is active.

Figure 3-1. Mac OS X Leopard's menu bar (with the Finder active)

As Figure 3-1 shows, the following menus and items can be found in the menu bar; each is covered later in this chapter:

- The Apple menu (1)
- The Application menu (2)
- A default set of application menus (3)
- Menu extras (4)
- The Accounts menu (5)
- Spotlight's search icon (6)

The Apple Menu

The Apple menu, which is displayed as an Apple symbol (⌘) in the menu bar, is completely different than in earlier versions of the Mac OS; you can no longer use it to store aliases for files, folders, or applications. The following is a list of what you'll find in Mac OS X's Apple menu:

About This Mac
This option pops open a window that gives you information about your Mac. Besides telling you that you're running Mac OS X on your computer, the window shows you which version of Mac OS X is installed, how much memory you have, and the speed and type of your processor.

Clicking on the More Info button launches the System Pro-filer (*/Applications/Utilities*), which tells you about your computer in greater detail.

Clicking on the version number in the About This Mac window reveals the build number of Mac OS X; click it again and you'll see the hardware serial number for your computer. These small details are important to have handy when contacting Apple Customer Service and when reporting a probable bug.

TIP

In earlier versions of the Mac OS, the About box changed depending on which application was active. For information about the application, you now have to go to the Application menu (located to the right of the Apple menu) and select the About option.

Software Update

This launches the Software Update preferences panel and checks for updates for Mac OS X and other Apple soft-ware installed on your system.

Mac OS X Software

This option takes you to Apple's Mac OS X page (*http:// www.apple.com/macosx*) in your default web browser.

System Preferences

This launches the System Preferences application, which replaces most of the control panels from earlier versions of the Mac OS. It provides a quick runthrough of the var-ious System Preferences panels.

Dock

This menu offers a quick way to change settings for the Dock (described in the section "The Dock," later in this chapter).

Location

This is similar to the Location Manager Control Panel from earlier versions of the Mac OS: it allows you to change locations quickly for connecting to a network and/or the Internet.

Recent Items

This menu option provides you with a list of the Recent Applications, Recent Documents, and Recent Servers you've accessed. The Clear Menu option allows you to reset the recent items from the menu.

Force Quit

Thanks to Mac OS X's protected memory, you don't have to restart the entire system if an application crashes or freezes. Instead, you can use this menu option (or Option-⌘-Esc) to open a window that lists the applications running on your system. To force quit an application, simply click on the application name, then click Force Quit.

TIP

Unlike with applications, you cannot force quit the Finder by Control-clicking its Dock icon. Instead, you need to re-launch the Finder. When you select the Finder, the Force Quit button changes to Relaunch; click that button to re-start the Finder.

Sleep

Selecting this option puts your Mac immediately into Sleep mode. This is different than the settings you dictate in System Preferences → Energy Saver for autosleep functionality. To "wake" your computer from Sleep mode, simply press any key.

Restart

This restarts your Mac. If any applications are running, the system quits them prior to shutting down. If an application has a window with unsaved changes, you are prompted to save changes before the application quits.

Shut Down

This shuts down your Mac. You can also shut down your Mac by pressing the Power-On button, which opens a dialog box with the options for restarting, shutting down, or putting your Mac to sleep.

Log Out

This option logs you out of your system and takes you back to your login screen. The keyboard shortcut to log out is Shift-⌘-Q.

The Application Menu

Immediately to the right of the Apple menu in the menu bar is the Application menu, shown in Figure 3-2. While the Apple menu contains commands relevant to the whole system, the Application menu—which is rendered in boldface with the name of the active application—contains commands relevant to the active application (but not to any of its windows or documents).

Figure 3-2. The Finder's Application menu

The following are some of the typical Application menu commands:

About Application Name

Displays a small window that typically features the application's name, icon, version number, authors, copyright information, web links, and whatever else the developers felt appropriate.

Preferences...

Calls up the application's preferences window. The standard keyboard shortcut to open an application's preferences window is ⌘- , (Command-comma).

Services

Brings up the Services submenu, covered in the section "The Services Menu," later in this chapter.

Hide Application Name

> Makes the application and all its windows (including minimized windows on the Dock) invisible and brings the next active application to the foreground. Clicking the application's Dock icon (or bringing forth any of its individual windows through its Dock menu) reveals the application once again. The standard keyboard shortcut for hiding an application is ⌘-H.

Hide Others

> Hides all running applications except the current one. The standard keyboard shortcut to hide other applications is Option-⌘-H.

Show All

> Reveals all hidden applications.

Quit Application Name

> Quits the application. The standard keyboard shortcut to quit an application is ⌘-Q.

Standard Application Menus

In addition to the Application menu, each application (including the Finder) has at least four additional menus in the menu bar:

File

> This menu contains commands for opening, creating, and saving files.

Edit

> This menu contains commands for working with files, including Copy, Cut, Paste, and the all-important Undo.

Window

> This menu not only keeps track of the windows an application has open, but it has options for minimizing and hiding windows as well.

Help

This menu varies greatly among applications. Some applications offer just a single command, Application Help (Shift-⌘-?), which either displays the application's documentation in the Apple Help Center or performs an action of the application's own choosing.

The Help menu in Mac OS X Leopard now has a Search field, which helps you find specific menu items in the application you're using. For example, let's say that you're using Safari and you want to find which menu contains options for bookmarks because you need help with exporting yours. Hit Shift-⌘-? to open the Help menu, and type "bookmark" in the Search field. You'll see a list pop in beneath the Search field that gives the various menu options that contain that text string. If you move the mouse over one of the items, or scroll down in the list with the Down or Up Arrow keys on your keyboard, you'll see something really cool. The appropriate menu pops open, and a floating arrow appears next to the menu option, as shown in Figure 3-3.

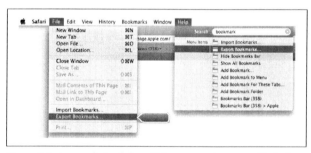

Figure 3-3. Leopard's beefed-up Help menu assists you with finding menu options based on keyword searching

Menu Extras

Mac OS X programs and services can place menu extras on the right side of the menu bar. Like the Apple menu, these little symbols remain constant regardless of which application you're using.

The menu extras' functions are typically reflected in their appearance, and they often carry menus loaded with commands, similar to other menus. Figure 3-4 shows the Bluetooth menu extra.

Figure 3-4. The Bluetooth menu extra

The Bluetooth menu extra can be added to the menu bar from the Bluetooth preference panel (System Preferences → Bluetooth → turn on the checkbox next to "Show Bluetooth status in the menu bar"). The Bluetooth menu extra mimics many of the functions of the Bluetooth preference panel, shows you which Bluetooth devices are within range, and offers a quick way to launch the Bluetooth File Exchange utility (*/Applications/Utilities*).

You can move a menu extra to a different location in the menu bar by Command-clicking the icon and dragging it left or right. As you move it around, the other menu extras move out of the way to make room. When you let go of the mouse button, the menu extra takes its new place in the menu bar. To remove a menu extra from the menu bar, Command-click on the icon, drag it off the menu bar, and let go of the mouse button.

TIP

Executables for most of the standard menu extras can be found in */System/Library/CoreServices/Menu Extras* as folders with *.menu* extensions.

Since Mac OS X's various applications and preference panes are covered throughout this book, the ones that offer menu extras are called out in their respective descriptions.

The Accounts Menu

One of the many new features added to Mac OS X Panther was something called Fast User Switching. This lets you have multiple users logged into the system at the same time.

If your Mac has more than one user account (set up via System Preferences → Accounts), you can turn on Fast User Switching, as well as specify which user the system automatically logs in to at startup. When you enable Fast User Switching, the Accounts menu appears at the far-right corner of the menu bar. This menu, shown in Figure 3-5, lists the user accounts on your Mac.

To switch to another user account, simply click on the bold-faced name of the user currently logged in and select another user account name from the Accounts menu. A login window appears that prompts you for the selected user's password. If your Mac supports Quartz Extreme, your display then rotates with a 3D cube effect to the other user's desktop.

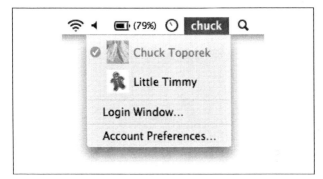

Figure 3-5. The Accounts menu

TIP

You are required to enter a password each time you switch user accounts from the Accounts menu.

The Application Switcher

One quick way to switch between running applications—without ever moving your hands from the keyboard—is to hold down the Command key (⌘) and then press the Tab key. This pops open the Application Switcher (shown in Figure 3-6), which displays the icons for all the applications you have running. You'll notice, too, that there's a little white box surrounding an application icon.

The first time you press the ⌘-Tab shortcut, that box surrounds the application you were previously using. If you continue pressing the Tab key while still holding down the ⌘ key, the white box moves right, to the next application in line. When you get to the end of the line, the box jumps to the first icon in the Application Switcher window and continues cycling through the icons until you stop pressing the Tab key.

Figure 3-6. Here you can see that the Application Switcher pops up on top of all other running applications; continue holding down the Command key and press the Tab key to select an application, then let go of the keys to bring that app to the front

When you let go of the ⌘-Tab keys, the application whose icon was surrounded by the white box is brought to the front so you can work with that app.

TIP

The Application Switcher is particularly helpful for times when you need to copy and paste information from one application into another. Just hit ⌘-Tab and quickly let go of the keys to switch applications in an instant. To switch back, hit ⌘-Tab again.

You can also add the Shift key to this combination (Shift-⌘-Tab) to make the little white box in the Application Switcher move backward (left) through the application icons. Here are a couple more tricks:

- Use the ⌘-Tab shortcut to open the Application Switcher, then move the mouse pointer over the application icons. As the mouse moves over each icon, the white box jumps to that icon. If you click on the icon, that app comes to the front and the Application Switcher disappears.

- With the Application Switcher open, press the Tab key to highlight an application. Continue holding the ⌘ key down and then press either Q to quit the application, H to hide the application, or W to close the topmost window for the application. Of course, you realize—since you're holding the ⌘ key down anyway—this is just like having that application in the foreground and pressing ⌘-Q for quit, ⌘-W to close a window, or ⌘-H to hide the application.

TIP

Now don't get too far ahead of yourself by thinking you can issue any keyboard shortcut while you're in the Application Switcher. These (Q, W, and H) are the only three application-related keyboard shortcuts that work within the Application Switcher. For example, you can't press N (⌘-N) and expect a new Safari window to pop open, or O (⌘-O) to open a Word document, or P (⌘-P) to print what's in an application's window while you're in the Application Switcher. To use these commands, or to do any other application-specific tasks, you'll first need to bring the respective application to the front.

Window Controls

Windows in Mac OS X have an entirely different set of controls than those from earlier versions of the Mac OS. These new window features are highlighted in Figure 3-7.

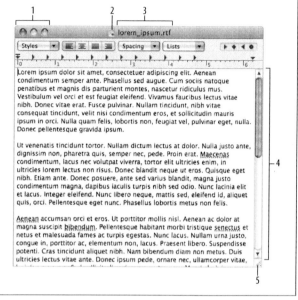

Figure 3-7. Standard window controls in Mac OS X

The following list identifies the controls:

- Close (red), Minimize (yellow), and Zoom/Maximize (green) window buttons (1)
- Proxy icon (2)
- Filename (3)
- Scrollbars and scroll arrows (4)
- Resize window control (5)

The top part of the window is known as the *title bar*. The title bar is home to the three colored window-control buttons for closing (red), minimizing (yellow), and zooming (green) the window. When you move your mouse over the buttons, you'll notice that they take on a different appearance, becoming an ×, a minus sign (–), or a plus sign (+). These are visual cues indicating the function that button performs:

- Clicking the × (the red button) closes the window.
- Clicking the – (the yellow button) minimizes the window.
- Clicking the + (the green button) makes the window bigger.

With some applications, such as TextEdit or Microsoft Word, you'll notice that the red close-window button may have a dark-colored dot in its center. This little dot means the document you're working on has unsaved changes. If you save the document by selecting File → Save (⌘-S), the dot disappears.

Window Tips

The following are tips for working with windows:

Open a new window?
    File → Open (⌘-O).

Close a window?
    File → Close (⌘-W).

Close all open windows for an application?
    Option-click on the red close-window button.

TIP

If there are changes that need to be saved in any of the windows being closed, you are prompted to save them. Either hit Return to save the changes, or ⌘-D to invoke the Don't Save button. As mentioned previously, in some applications, a quick way to tell whether a window has unsaved changes is to look at the red close-window button; if there is a dark-red circle in its center, the document needs to be saved.

Minimize a window?

    Click on the yellow minimize button.

    Window → Minimize Window (⌘-M).

    Double-click on the window's title bar.

Minimize all open windows for a single application?

    Option-⌘-M.

TIP

With some applications, Option-⌘-M might function differently. For example, issuing Option-⌘-M in Microsoft Word opens the Paragraph format window (Format → Paragraph). Other applications that won't minimize all of the windows with this shortcut include the iChat, Quick-Time Player, Terminal, and TextEdit. To be safe, you should save changes to the file before trying to minimize all the application's windows with Option-⌘-M.

Quickly create an alias of an open file, or move it, depending on the app (e.g., Word)?

    Click and drag the file's proxy icon to a new location (i.e., the Desktop, Dock, Finder, etc.). The file must first be saved and named before an alias can be created.

TIP

Dragging a folder's proxy icon from a Finder window's title bar moves that folder to the new location instead of creating an alias. If you want to create an alias for a folder, you should select the folder in the Finder, hold down the Option-⌘ keys, and then drag the folder to where you'd like the alias to be. As a visual cue to let you know you're creating an alias, the mouse pointer changes to a curved arrow.

Find out where a file exists in the filesystem?

    Command-click on the proxy icon. This pops open a context menu showing you where the file exists. If you select another item (such as a hard drive or a folder) from the proxy icon's context menu, a Finder window opens, taking you to that location.

Hide the windows for other active applications?

Option-⌘-click on the Dock icon for the application you're using; all open windows for the other applications instantly disappear. To bring another application's windows to the front, click on that application's Dock icon; to unhide all the other windows, select Show All from the application menu of the application you're currently using (for example, select Finder → Show All).

Quickly switch from one application window to another?

Use the ⌘-` keyboard shortcut (that's a backtick, not an apostrophe). For example, if you have two Word documents open and you want to switch to the other document window after copying something, just hit ⌘-` and the other Word document window comes to the front.

The Dock

The Dock in Mac OS X Leopard has received a facelift, getting a new flashy design and added features that allow you to quickly access files on your Mac. The Dock, shown in Figure 3-8, holds application aliases, making it easy for you to quickly launch programs with a single mouse click. To launch an application in the Dock, simply click the icon. While the application is starting, its icon bounces in the Dock; after it starts, a light-blue dot appears below the icon to indicate that the application is running.

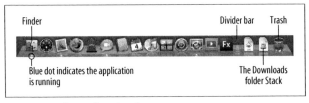

Figure 3-8. The Dock and its features

If you look closely at Figure 3-8, you'll notice that the Dock is split into two parts by a dashed bar that looks similar to the lane markers in the road. On the left of this line, you will find application icons for the Finder, Spaces, Time Machine, Safari, Mail, iChat, Preview, iTunes, Address Book, and iCal. To the right, you'll see a quick link to the Downloads folder (which resides in your Home folder), and the Trash. If you aren't sure which application an icon relates to, simply move your mouse over the icon, and a balloon appears telling you what the application is, as shown in Figure 3-9.

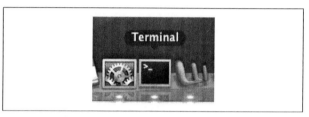

Figure 3-9. When you move your mouse over a Dock icon, a bubble appears to tell you which application the icon relates to

If you need to use an application that isn't in the Dock, open a Finder window by clicking its icon at the far left of the Dock (the blue smiley-face icon). If you're already in the Finder, you can quickly get to the Applications folder by using its keyboard shortcut, Shift-⌘-A, or by clicking the Applications quick link in the Places section of the sidebar. To launch the application, simply double-click the application's icon.

To add an application icon to the Dock, simply drag its icon from the Finder to the left side of the Dock's divider bar and let go. To remove an application, click on the icon and hold the mouse button down, then drag the icon away from the Dock; the icon disappears in a puff of smoke.

Stacks

One of the coolest new features added to Mac OS X Leopard's Dock is a thing called Stacks. Whenever you place a folder in the Dock next to the Trash icon, the contents of that folder turn into a Stack. They're called Stacks because the icons for the items in the folder are stacked one on top of the other, sort of like a pile of photographs you need to file away.

When you first install Mac OS X Leopard, you already have one Stack folder in the Dock, the Downloads folder. Whenever you download something from the Internet, such as a disk image for an application or a PDF file, those items are automatically stored in your Downloads folder, which resides within your Home folder. To add more folders as Stacks to your Dock, simply open a new Finder window (⌘-N), locate the folder you want to become a Stack (such as your Documents folder or a folder containing your favorite photographs), and drag that to the right side of the Dock near the Trash. An alias of that folder is created in the Dock, and it instantly turns into a viewable Stack.

To quickly see and access the files in a Stack, simply click on the stack, and a list of files pops out of the Dock (as shown in Figure 3-10 for the Downloads folder). To open a file, simply move your mouse over the file of your choice and click once. The Stack springs back into the Dock, and the file opens using the appropriate application.

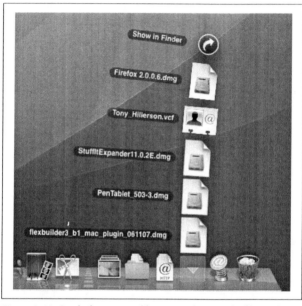

Figure 3-10. Stacks let you quickly view and access the files within a folder

If you place a folder that contains image files on the right side of the Dock's divider, you will see thumbnails of the images, as shown in Figure 3-11. To open one of the images, simply move the mouse over the image and click its icon.

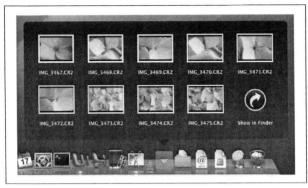

Figure 3-11. If you place a Stack folder that contains image files in the Dock, image icons are displayed so you can quickly choose the image you want

---

TIP

To change the appearance of the Stack, Control-click on it and select View as → Fan or Grid.

Dock Menus

Every active application icon has a *Dock menu*, which you can call up by either Control-clicking the icon or clicking on the icon and holding the mouse button down. An application's Dock menu is attached to its icon, as shown in Figure 3-12.

Dock menus contain, as commands, the titles of all the windows an application has open, each of which is marked with a little "window" symbol. Select one to bring it forth along with its parent application. The top window will have a checkmark next to it; there is no distinction for minimized windows.

Figure 3-12. A typical Dock menu; this one for Microsoft Word includes a list of open document windows

Every application's Dock menu typically contains at least a couple of other commands, including:

Keep in Dock

This option appears only for icons whose applications aren't permanently placed in the Dock. Normally, the icon of an undocked application vanishes once you quit the application. If you select this option, the application's icon gets a permanent home in the Dock.

Remove from Dock

This removes an application's icon from the Dock. If the application is already running, the icon is removed from the Dock when you quit that application.

Open at Login

When selected, this option sets the application to launch automatically each time you log in to your user account.

Show In Finder

Opens a Finder window showing the location of the application on your system.

Quit

Quits the application, even if it's not in the foreground. The application reacts as if you had selected Quit from its application menu or used the keyboard shortcut ⌘-Q to quit the application.

If you hold down the Option key while looking at an application's Dock menu, Quit changes to Force Quit; selecting this option kills that application instantly.

The Finder's icon lacks a Quit or Force Quit option. (In fact, all it has is a list of open Finder windows and a Hide option to hide all open Finder windows.) If you need to restart the Finder for some odd reason, do so by selecting → Force Quit (Option-⌘-Escape). Then, select the Finder and click on the Relaunch button, as described earlier in this chapter in the section "The Apple Menu."

Using and Configuring the Dock

Here are some helpful hints and tips for using and configuring your Dock:

Quickly resize the Dock without launching its System Preferences panel?

Place the mouse over the divider bar in the Dock; the pointer changes from an arrow to a horizontal bar with arrows pointing up and down. Click on the divider bar and move the mouse up or down to make the Dock larger or smaller, respectively.

Change the Dock's preferences?

 → Dock → Dock Preferences.

System Preferences → Dock.

Control-click on the Dock's divider bar and select Dock Preferences from the context menu.

Add a program to the Dock?

Drag and drop an application's icon from a Finder window into the Dock.

After launching an application that isn't normally in the Dock, Control-click on that application's icon and select "Keep in Dock" from the pop-up menu.

Remove a program from the Dock?

Drag the application icon from the Dock and drop it anywhere.

Change the Dock's location from the bottom of the screen to the left or right side?

System Preferences → Dock → Position on screen.

 → Dock → Position on (Left, Bottom, or Right).

Control-click on the Dock's divider → Position on screen → (Left, Bottom, or Right).

Control the magnification of icons in the Dock?

System Preferences → Dock → Magnification.

 → Dock → Turn Magnification (On/Off).

Control-click the Dock's divider and select Turn Magnification (On/Off).

Hide the Dock when I'm not using it?

Option-⌘-D.

System Preferences → Dock → Automatically hide and show the Dock.

 → Dock → Turn Hiding (On/Off).

Control-click the Dock's divider and select Turn Hiding (On/Off).

Stop application icons from bouncing when a program is launched?

System Preferences → Dock → uncheck the checkbox next to "Animate opening applications." Instead of the application's icon bouncing, the little blue dot beneath the application icon pulses as the program launches.

Create a new Stack in the Dock, showing the pictures in my Pictures folder?

Go to Finder → Home → Pictures, and then drag your Pictures folder to the right side of the Dock, near the Trash.

Dock Tricks

The following key-mouse commands can be used when clicking on an icon in the Dock:

Command-click

If you ⌘-click an application icon in the Dock (or just click and hold down the mouse button), the Finder opens, taking you to that application's folder.

Shift-⌘-click

Opens a Finder window to the application's location in the filesystem. This is similar to Control-clicking a Dock icon and selecting Show In Finder from its context menu.

Control-click

If you Control-click a running application in the Dock (or click and hold down the mouse button), a pop-up menu opens, listing the windows that the application has open, as well as options to show the application in the Finder and to Quit the application.

If you press the Option key while Control-clicking an icon in the Dock, the Quit option toggles to Force Quit.

Shift-click

If you Shift-click on a Stack in the Dock, the Stack opens slowly, just like Shift-clicking a window's yellow minimize button makes it retreat to the Dock slowly.

Option-click

Option-clicking has the same effect as Control-clicking, with one exception: Quit has been replaced by Force Quit in the pop-up menu.

Option-⌘-click

Hides the windows of all other open applications and switches (if necessary) to the clicked application; similar to selecting Hide Others from the application menu.

TIP

You can also empty the trash by clicking on the Trash icon in the Dock, holding down the mouse button, and selecting Empty Trash from the contextual menu that appears.

Trash

Regardless of how vast and expansive you think your hard drive is, eventually you're going to run out of space. When you do, the way you get rid of any unnecessary files is by moving them to the Trash. To move a file or folder to the Trash, you can either select the item in the Finder and drag it to the Trash icon in the Dock (see Figure 3-8) or quickly move it to the Trash by holding down the ⌘ key and hitting the Delete key (⌘-Delete). To see what's in your Trash, just click on the Trash icon in your Dock and a Finder window pops open, revealing what's inside.

TIP

If you happen to move the wrong file to the Trash and catch it right away, you can use Mac OS X's Undo short-cut (⌘-Z) to move the file back to where it belongs. Remember, though, you'll need to do this right away, because if you do anything else in the meantime, the Undo applies to your last action.

To empty the Trash, you can either go to the Finder's application menu and select Empty Trash (Finder → Empty Trash), or you can use Shift-⌘-Delete from within the Finder. If you've used the Finder's application menu, you've

---

probably noticed that there's another item there: Secure Empty Trash. If you select this item, any of the files currently residing in your Trash are permanently removed from your system. But what makes this secure? Well, it doesn't just delete the file once like the standard Empty Trash does; Secure Empty Trash deletes the file and writes over the space where the file once was—many times—making it nearly impossible for that file to ever be recovered.

WARNING

Yes, this means that even when you've selected Empty Trash, there is a chance someone can recover that trashed file for you. It's not easy, but it can be done. With Secure Empty Trash, however, the chances of recovering that file are nil, so make sure you really want to trash that file before selecting Secure Empty Trash.

In Mac OS X Tiger, you had to manually choose the Secure Empty Trash menu item; however, in Leopard, you can set this as your default method of trashing files. To do this, open a Finder window and open its preferences (Finder → Preferences, or ⌘-,), then click Advanced and turn on the checkbox next to "Empty Trash securely," as shown in Figure 3-13.

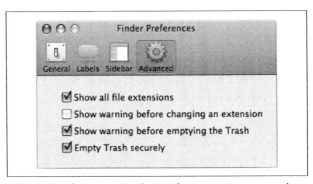

Figure 3-13. The "Empty Trash securely" option gives you another level of security on your Mac, but keep in mind that any files trashed that way won't be recoverable—ever

Now if you use the keyboard shortcut for emptying the trash, Secure Empty Trash will be used by default, which means anything you trash will be gone for good.

TIP

If you enable the "Empty Trash securely" feature in the Finder, you might consider leaving the option for "Show warning before emptying the Trash" checked as well. That way, each time you go to empty the Trash, you'll get a reminder that tells you the files will be securely removed from the system.

The Finder

Mac OS X's Finder is the main program you'll use for locating files and folders on your Mac. The Finder displays the contents of drives and folders, is used for mounting networked drives, and includes Spotlight to help you quickly find what you're looking for.

Leopard's Finder includes many new features, including Quick Look, Cover Flow View, a revamped Sidebar, changes to its preferences including the option to set Secure Empty Trash as the default...and the list goes on. Rather than spend a bunch of time talking about what's new, let's take a look.

Finder Basics

The Finder serves as a graphical file manager by offering four ways (or Views) to look at the files, folders, applications, and other filesystems (or volumes, such as your iDisk, a FireWire drive, or another Mac) mounted on your system. Its unique features are highlighted in Figure 3-14.

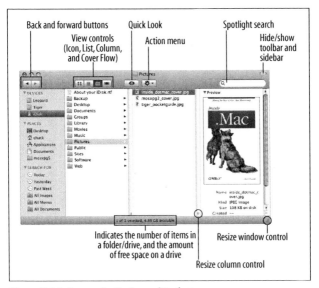

Back and forward buttons — Quick Look — Spotlight search

View controls (Icon, List, Column, and Cover Flow) — Action menu — Hide/show toolbar and sidebar

Indicates the number of items in a folder/drive, and the amount of free space on a drive — Resize window control

Resize column control

Figure 3-14. Leopard's Finder and its features

Mac OS X's Finder has three distinct features:

Toolbar

Located across the top of the Finder window, the toolbar offers buttons that let you go back or forward to a previous folder or view, buttons for changing the four different views (Icon, List, Column, or Cover Flow), buttons for Quick Look and the Action menu, and a Spotlight Search field for quickly finding files and folders on your Mac.

Sidebar

Located on the left edge of the Finder window, the Sidebar offers a split view for accessing drives and other items on your Mac. The Finder's Sidebar in Leopard is significantly different from earlier versions of Mac OS X, and it takes on the look and feel of iTunes' sidebar.

The Sidebar is organized into the following four sections:

Devices
> This section lists the various devices connected to your Mac, including your hard drive, iDisk (if you have a .Mac account), any connected USB or Fire-Wire drives, CDs or DVDs, and iPods.

Shared
> The Shared section lists any shared devices, e.g., another Mac you're connected to via Bonjour or a networked drive such as an AFP or SMB share.

Places
> These are places on your hard drive, such as folders for your Desktop, Home, Applications, and Documents. If there is a folder you need quick access to that isn't in this default list, just locate it in the Finder and drag it to the Places section in the sidebar.

Search For
> The Search For item helps you find files and folders that have changed recently (Today, Yesterday, and Past Week), and it also includes Smart Folders for gathering your images, movies, and documents together so you can quickly locate the file you're looking for.

You can further configure the Sidebar's settings by opening the Finder's preferences (Finder → Preferences, or ⌘-,) and clicking the Sidebar button. As shown in Figure 3-15, you will see a list of all the possible items that could show up in the Sidebar, and you have the option of toggling them on or off by clicking the checkboxes.

The View
> This area of the Finder is the big section to the right of the Sidebar. The View displays the contents of the drives and folders of your system. The default view is Icon View, which displays the files and folders as named icons;

however, you can change the view to List, Column, or Cover Flow View by clicking on the appropriate button in the toolbar.

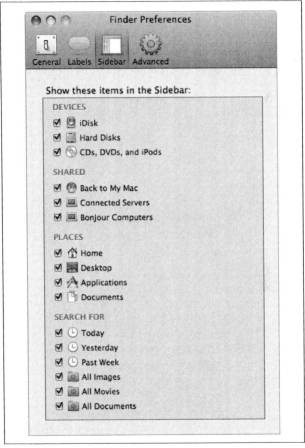

Figure 3-15. Use the checkboxes in the Sidebar preferences to determine what will show up in your Finder's Sidebar

To add a Sidebar shortcut for a file, folder, or application, drag the item's icon to the Places section of the Sidebar. When you need to open that item (or launch the application), all you need to do is click once on the icon, just as if it were in your Dock.

To remove an item from the Sidebar, simply drag the icon away from the Finder window and let go of the mouse button; the icon disappears with a poof.

More later on the Finder's Toolbar and on how to search with the Finder; for now, let's look at the four views available in the Finder.

Finder Views

As previously mentioned, the Finder has four different views for you to choose from. Each view has its own advantages. As you become more and more comfortable working with Mac OS X, you'll most likely find one that suits you best.

TIP

You can quickly change the Finder's viewpoint by using ⌘-1 for Icon View, ⌘-2 for List View, ⌘-3 for Column View, or ⌘-4 for Cover Flow View.

Icon View

The Icon View shows the contents of a directory as either a file, folder, or application icon, as shown in Figure 3-16. Double-clicking on an icon does one of three things:

- Launches an application
- Opens a file
- Displays the contents of a double-clicked folder in the Finder window

---

Figure 3-16. The Finder, in Icon View

Table 3-1 presents a list of keyboard shortcuts for use with the Finder's Icon View.

Table 3-1. Icon View's keyboard shortcuts

Key command	Description
Up, Down, Left, and Right Arrow	Move through the icons in the View according to the direction indicated on the key pressed.
Shift-Arrow	When one icon is selected and the Shift-Arrow (Up, Down, Left, or Right) keys are pressed, the icon in that direction will be selected as well.

List View

With List View, a directory's contents are displayed in a list, as shown in Figure 3-17. To display the contents of a folder, you can click on the disclosure triangle (the black triangle to the left of the folder, shown in the figure).

Another way to navigate through the icons and folders in the Finder's List View is by using the keyboard shortcuts listed in Table 3-2.

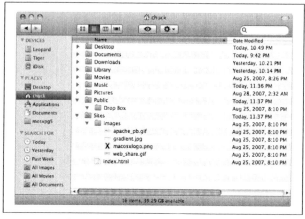

Figure 3-17. The Finder, in List View

Table 3-2. List View's keyboard shortcuts

Key command	Description
Down Arrow	Move down through the list of items.
Up Arrow	Move up through the list of items.
Right Arrow	Open a folder's disclosure triangle to reveal the folder's contents.
Left Arrow	Close a folder's disclosure triangle to hide the folder's contents.
Option-Right Arrow	Open a folder and any of its subfolders.
Option-Left Arrow	Close a folder and any of its subfolders.

To open all the folders in the View, select all the View's contents (⌘-A) and use Option-Right Arrow (likewise, use Option-Left Arrow to close them again). To open all the folders in the View, including subfolders, add the Shift key (Shift-Option-Right Arrow to open, Shift-Option-Left Arrow to close).

Column View

Column View, shown in Figure 3-18, displays a directory's contents in column form. This is similar to List View, except that when you click on an item, a new pane opens to the right and either exposes the contents of a folder or displays information (known as metadata) about a file, including its name, type, and file size.

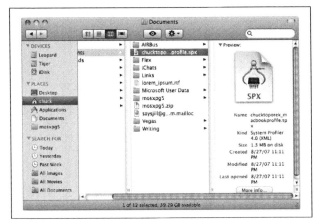

Figure 3-18. The Finder, in Column View

Table 3-3 lists the keyboard shortcuts for use with the Finder's Column View.

Table 3-3. Column View's keyboard shortcuts

Key command	Description
Up, Down, Left, Right Arrow	Move through the columns in the View according to the direction indicated on the key pressed.

Cover Flow View

New to the Finder in Leopard is the Cover Flow View, shown in Figure 3-19. Cover Flow first made its way to the Mac as a third-party plug-in for iTunes, until Apple acquired the company and made Cover Flow a permanent fixture in iTunes—as it has now for the Finder.

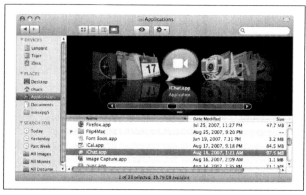

Figure 3-19. Leopard's Cover Flow displays an image of the file you've selected in the Finder, along with some basic file information in the pane beneath

The Finder's version of Cover Flow displays files and folders similar to the way iTunes displays cover art for the music in your collection. With the Finder, Cover Flow shows you the icons for a folder's files in a fanned-out view, as shown in Figure 3-19.

Table 3-4 lists the keyboard shortcuts for use with the Finder's Cover Flow View.

Table 3-4. Cover Flow View's keyboard shortcuts

Key command	Description
Right or Left Arrow	Use the Left and Right Arrow keys on your keyboard to fan through the icons.
⌘-Down Arrow	Opens a folder so you can see what's inside.
⌘-Up Arrow	Goes up in the directory path. For example, if you were in your Pictures folder and wanted to go back to your Home folder, you could use ⌘-Up Arrow.
⌘-[	Go back.
⌘-]	Go forward.

The Finder's Toolbar

Along the top of the Finder window is a toolbar (shown in Figure 3-14), which offers a quick way to switch between View modes and search for files on your Mac.

You can add a file, folder, or application to the Finder's toolbar by dragging and dropping its icon to the toolbar. Applications you add to the toolbar launch with a single click, just as they do in the Dock; files open in their respective application, and folders open in a new Finder window. To remove an item you've placed in the Finder's toolbar, hold down the ⌘ key, click on the item, and drag the item off the toolbar; it disappears in a poof.

Hiding the toolbar

Located at the upper-right corner of the Finder window is an elliptical button that can be used to hide the Finder's toolbar, as shown in Figure 3-20.

Figure 3-20. The Finder window with the toolbar and Sidebar hidden

In Leopard, when you click on the Hide/Show toolbar button, the Finder's toolbar behaves differently than in earlier versions of Mac OS X. If you click this button, the paned view in the Sidebar goes away. Click the button again, and the Finder reverts to its former self. If you are in Icon or List View with the toolbar hidden, the Finder window performs just like Mac OS 9's Finder windows. Double-clicking on a folder icon opens a new window for that folder, displaying its contents. The Column View and Cover Flow View function similarly, as shown earlier in Figures 3-18 and 3-19, respectively.

Customizing the toolbar

In addition to adding shortcuts to files, folders, and applications, you can also customize the toolbar in other ways. For example, if you don't like the current arrangement of buttons in the toolbar, you can ⌘-click on a button and drag it left or right. If you drag a button off the toolbar, it disappears with a poof.

Another way to customize the Finder's toolbar is either to select View → Customize Toolbar, or Option-⌘-click on the toolbar button. A sheet flops out of the Finder's title bar, revealing a host of other buttons you can add to the toolbar. To add a new button, just drag the item to the toolbar and place it wherever you'd like. When you've finished configuring the toolbar to your liking, click Done.

The Action Menu

The Finder's Action menu (the one that looks like a little gear wheel), is shown in Figure 3-21. If you click on a file or folder in the Finder and then click on the Action menu, a pop-up menu appears, which lets you do any of the following:

- Create a New Folder within the selected folder, or within the same folder if the item selected is a file.
- Create a New Burn Folder, which can be burned to CD or DVD later without having to use Disk Utility.

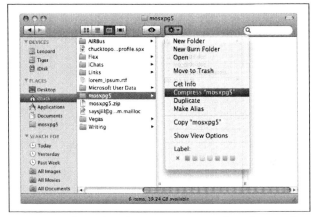

Figure 3-21. The Finder's Action menu gives you lots of options for tasks that you'd otherwise have to go back up to the menu bar to use

- Open the selected item. Files open in their associated application (for example, Word files open in Microsoft Word, HTML files open in Safari, etc.), and folders open in a new Finder window; if the selected item is an application icon, the application opens.

- Move to Trash moves the selected item to the trash so you can delete (or recover) it later.

- Open the Get Info window to see details about the selected item.

- Compress lets you create a zipped archive of the selected file or folder. This is particularly handy when you want to quickly create a ZIP archive of only a few files within a folder.

  If you've only selected one file to zip, the Finder creates a *.zip* file, retaining the original filename (for example, if you select *myfile.txt* and select Create Archive, the zipped file is named *myfile.txt.zip*). However, if you select more than one file, the zipped file is given the generic name of

Archive.zip; you'll need to change the name of the file if you want it to be something recognizable (such as *myworkfiles.zip*).

TIP

⌘-click the files you want to archive, then select Create Archive from the Action menu. To unzip an archive, just double-click the ZIP file to unpack it in the Finder.

• Duplicate the selected item. This creates an exact duplicate of the item you've selected and tacks on the word "copy" to its filename (for example, if you make a duplicate of *myfile.txt*, its copy of that file is named *myfile copy.txt*).

TIP

Another option for making a duplicate of a file is to first select the file in the Finder and then use the ⌘-D keyboard shortcut.

Keep in mind that this is much different from using the same keyboard shortcut within an Open or Save dialog box (which switches from its present disk location to the Desktop so you can open or save a file there).

• The Make Alias option lets you create an alias (sort of a shortcut or symbolic link) of the item, which you can then place elsewhere on your Mac.

For example, say you have a folder named Home Movies inside your Movies folder. To get to that folder, you need to open a Finder window, select Movies from the Sidebar (or from your Home folder), and then select the Home Movies folder. Wouldn't it be easier if you just had an icon for the Home Movies folder on your Desktop, which you could double-click to open the actual folder? If you select the Home Movies folder in the Finder, and select Make Alias, an alias of that folder is created there.

Now all you need to do is drag that aliased folder to your Desktop, and your life suddenly gets easier.

- The Copy item is used to copy and paste files (or a folder and its contents) from one location to another. When you use Copy, it creates a copy of the selected item and keeps that in the system's pasteboard. To actually make the copy of the selected items appear, go to another folder (such as your Desktop) and select Edit → Paste (or ⌘-V) to paste a copy of the item in the new location. You can even use this option to copy and paste a file or folder into an email message in Mail.

- Show View Options is only available when you've selected an item in the Finder's Sidebar, but nothing in the View area. When selected, this opens a palette window, which you can use to adjust the settings for that particular Finder View. Once you've changed the View's settings, click the red close-window button to close the palette. Any future Finder windows of that View type will use the settings you've applied.

- Finally, you'll see an × followed by a row of gumdrop-like colored dots at the very bottom of the Action menu. These are color Labels, which you can apply to any item you select in the Finder. (The × turns the Label off for the selected item.) When you apply a Label to an item, the name of the item is colored with the color of your choice. Labels can be used for anything your little heart desires, from colorizing your hard drive to prioritizing project folders. Labels can even be assigned a name, using the Labels pane of the Finder's preferences (Finder → Preferences → Labels).

- The Quick Look option is available when you've selected more than one file. For example, if you select a bunch of images in a folder, you can click the Action menu and select Quick Look *X* Items, and those files will pop open in Quick Look, as shown in Figure 3-22.

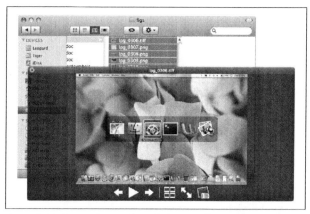

Figure 3-22. Leopard's Quick Look feature offers a great way to preview files and images; move your mouse to the bottom of the Quick Look display to use the controls: back, play/pause, forward, index sheet, full-screen, or add to iPhoto if the selected items are images

If you select some images (such as those in your Pictures folder) in the Finder, try holding down the Option key while looking at the Quick Look icon. You'll notice that the Quick Look icon changes to what looks like a Play button. Rather than displaying the images in a Quick Look window, the images are displayed in a Slideshow, as shown in Figure 3-23.

While in the Slideshow, the images are displayed in full-screen mode. If you move the mouse, you will see the head-up display (HUD) controls along the bottom of the slideshow (the HUD controls are circled in Figure 3-23). To exit the Slideshow, click the × icon at the far right of the HUD.

Figure 3-23. From Quick Look to a full-screen Slideshow, just by holding down the Option key and clicking the Slideshow button (which used to be the Quick Look button)

NOTE

According to Wikipedia (*http://en.wikipedia.org*), a "head-up display," or HUD, is "any transparent display that presents data without obstructing the user's view. Although they were initially developed for military aviation, HUDs are now used in commercial aircraft, automobiles, and other applications." Just another way of showing that Mac OS X is on the cutting-edge of application design.

Searching from the Finder

As shown earlier in Figure 3-14, the Finder's toolbar includes a Search field, which uses Spotlight to help you quickly find what you're looking for. As soon as you start typing something into the Search field, Spotlight jumps into action and starts searching, as shown in Figure 3-24.

Figure 3-24. When you are searching from the Finder, Spotlight takes over and starts finding files as soon as you type something in the Search field

As you can see from Figure 3-24, the Finder view area changes to show you the results. Along the top, you'll see buttons that let you apply the search to "This Mac" (which searches every file on the system), or just your user account name. If you look to the far right, you will see a Save button that lets you save your search as a Smart Folder. To add additional options to your search criteria, click the Add (+) button to the right of Save.

TIP

If you find yourself doing the same search over and over again, you really should consider clicking that Save button. All you'll need to do the next time around is select the Smart Folder in the Finder's Sidebar, and your results instantly come into the Finder view.

Finder Tips

The following are some tips for working with the Finder:

Hide the Finder toolbar and Sidebar?
> View → Hide Toolbar (Option-⌘-T).
>
> Click on the transparent button in the upper-right corner of the title bar.

Customize the Finder toolbar?
> Finder → View → Customize Toolbar.
>
> Option-⌘-click the toolbar button.
>
> Control-click within the toolbar and select Customize Toolbar from the context menu.

Show only the icons or text labels of items in the toolbar?
> View → Customize Toolbar → Show → select Icon & Text from the pull-down menu.

Locate a specific folder in the Finder?
> Go → Go to Folder (or Shift-⌘-G).

TIP

You can use Shift-⌘-G to go to directories such as */usr* and */bin*, which are part of Mac OS X's Unix filesystem.

Search for hidden dot files on my system?
> Open a Finder window and follow these steps:
>
> 1. Select File → Find from the menu bar, or use the keyboard shortcut, ⌘-F.
>
> 2. From the first pop-up menu, select Name, and in the field next to "contains," enter the word for which you'd like to search. For this example, type in *bash*.
>
> 3. Click the Add (+) button at the far right. This adds another row to give you more search options.

4. Click the first pop-up menu in the second row, which should be "What" by default. Go down in the menu and select "Other." In the sheet that slides down, type in the word "visible" in the Search field. You will see the item, "File invisible" as the only item you can choose. Click the checkbox in the "In Menu" column to add this option to the search menu, and then click OK.

5. In the second pop-up menu of the second row, select "Invisible Items." You should see file *.bash_history* show up in the search results, as shown in Figure 3-25.

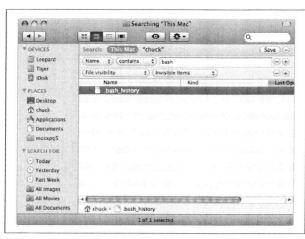

Figure 3-25. Searching with the Finder can even help you locate hidden (or invisible) files on your system

---

TIP

You can force the Finder to view Unix directories by using the Go → Go to Folder (Shift-⌘-G) option and entering a Unix filesystem path (such as */etc*).

Creating New Folders

Folders. Seems like a pretty simple concept, doesn't it? Well, now with Mac OS X Leopard, you have options for creating three different types of folders:

- Regular folders
- Smart Folders
- Burn Folders

Everybody's used to creating a folder; you either select File → New Folder or use the Shift-⌘-N keyboard shortcut in the Finder. But now with Leopard, you have the option to create Smart Folders and Burn Folders anywhere you'd like.

Smart Folders have been around since Panther, but they've also been used in applications such as iTunes and iPhoto. To create a Smart Folder, select File → New Smart Folder (or Option-⌘-N). For an example of how to put Smart Folders to good use, see the section "Mail.app" in Chapter 6. When you save a Smart Folder, you are also given the option of having it show up in the Finder's Sidebar, in the Search For section. If you know this is something you'll use often, make sure you click that checkbox before saving the Smart Folder.

TIP

The Smart Folders you create are saved in *~/Library/Saved Searches* as files with a *.savedSearch* file extension. While the *.savedSearch* files appear as a folder in the Finder, they are merely XML files that contain a query for the search data and location.

Burn Folders offer a quick and easy way for you to burn files to CD or DVD. To create a Burn Folder, just select File → New Burn Folder (there is no keyboard shortcut), give the folder a name (such as *mybitchinburnfolder.fpbf*), and then start dragging files into it. The files you place in the Burn Folder are actually aliased to the original file. To burn your

Burn Folder to CD or DVD, just select the Burn Folder in the Finder (you'll see a dark-gray bar appear above the filel-ist in the Finder, as shown in Figure 3-26), and then click the Burn button.

Figure 3-26. Burn Folders have an .fpbf file extension; when they're selected in the Finder, a gray bar appears below the toolbar

The Services Menu

The Services menu is available as a submenu in the Applica-tion menu of most Mac OS X applications. It allows the fore-ground application to invoke functions of other applications, usually while passing along user-selected text or objects to them.

The Services menu's contents depend on the applications installed on your Mac and the services they offer to other applications. When installed, some applications such as Mail, Safari, and BBEdit place entries in the Services menu.

If an application provides more than one service, those items are placed into a submenu named after that application. For example, Mail offers two services, Send Selection and Send To, as shown in Figure 3-27.

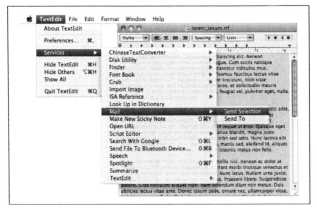

Figure 3-27. Mail's options in the Services menu let you send text selections in an email message

With some text selected in a TextEdit document (as shown in Figure 3-27), select TextEdit (the Application menu) → Services → Mail → Send Selection. Mac OS X copies that text and places it in the body of a new message in Mail. Then all you need to do is enter the email address of the person to whom you want to send the text, enter a subject line, and click the Send button. (The Services → Mail → Send To option places the selected item in an email message's To field.)

TIP

Some services also offer keyboard shortcuts, which makes it easy to send selected text to a Bluetooth device (Shift-⌘-B) or to create a new sticky note (Shift-⌘-Y).

Exposé

If you've ever wished for a quick way to get at your desktop, or just at the windows for a single application, Exposé is your answer. Exposé (shown in Figure 3-28) uses Quartz Extreme to make accessing windows—and your desktop—a dream come true.

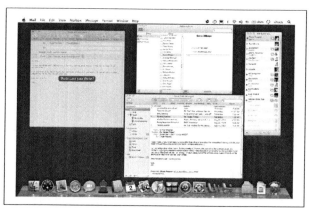

Figure 3-28. Exposé in action

Exposé runs in the background and is configurable through its System Preferences panel (System Preferences → Dashboard & Exposé). The keyboard shortcuts for Exposé are listed in Table 3-5.

Table 3-5. Keyboard shortcuts for Exposé

Key command	Description
F9	Spreads out all open windows so they're viewable on the desktop.
F10	Separates just the application windows (not including the Finder windows) so they're viewable on the desktop.
F11	Clears all of the windows away from the desktop so you can see what's there.

After using one of Exposé's keyboard shortcuts, you can either click on the window you'd like to bring forward or use the arrow keys on your keyboard to move around; to select a window, hit the Return key.

TIP

It's worth noting, however, that if you have Spaces enabled, Exposé only affects the windows in the active Space. For example, if you hit F9 to spread out the windows with Exposé in a Space that has Mail, iChat, and Address Book open (as shown in Figure 3-28), and you have iCal running in another Space, and Safari in a third Space, then only the Mail, iChat, and Address Book windows will spread out; you won't see the iCal or Safari windows.

Using the Dashboard & Exposé preferences panel (System Preferences → Dashboard & Exposé), you can set Hot Corners for performing the actions of the function keys, or change the key settings to some other key combination. Hot Corners allow you to set the corners of your screen as special "hot" points, which invoke some action when you move your mouse there. For example, you could set the upper-left corner to enable Exposé's All Windows option, and the lower-left corner to Show Desktop, which scoots all open windows off-screen temporarily so you can see what's on the desktop.

The Dashboard

The Dashboard offers a set of mini-applications, known as Widgets, that provide you with easy access to information when you need it. The beauty of Dashboard Widgets is that they're small, they don't take up very much of your Mac's system resources (memory and CPU power), and best of all, they're only in your face when you need them.

The Widgets that come preinstalled with Mac OS X Leopard include:

Address Book
> Provides an interface to the contacts stored in your Address Book application.

Business
> Finds local businesses and organizations. Need to find the phone number for Bill & Ted's Excellent Pizza? Let the Business Widget do the walking for you.

Calculator
> Works as a simple calculator for doing basic math.

Dictionary/Thesaurus/Apple
> Acts as either a dictionary, a thesaurus, or a directory to Apple terms (new for Leopard), depending on which item you select in the Widget's "title bar." To use this multifunction Widget, just select the desired function and type a word into the Search field, and you'll soon see a definition of the word and/or a list of synonyms.

ESPN
> This Widget lets you quickly access game scores and the latest sports news headlines, fed from ESPN.com.

Flight Tracker
> Uses the Web to help you track the progress of any flight on most major airlines around the world.

Google
> This provides you with a simple Search field for searching on Google. Just type in your search string and hit Return, and the search results show up in your default web browser.

iCal
> Despite its name, this only lets you view a simple calendar, showing you the date and a view of the current month. Unfortunately, this Widget does not pull in information from your iCal calendars or to-do lists.

iTunes

When iTunes is running, this Widget provides a very slick interface for operating iTunes. The interface for the iTunes Widget is very similar to that for the DVD Player application (*/Applications*).

Movies

Helps you find local movie listings in your area.

People

Need to look up someone's phone number in the phone book, but don't have a copy of the White Pages available? Fret no more—the People Widget will help you find the person if he's listed in the local phone directory.

Ski Report

This Widget pulls together weather reports and ski conditions from the local slopes.

Stickies

Lets you create Stickies notes, which you can use to quickly get at information you need. These Stickies are separate from those you create with Mac OS X's Stickies application (*/Applications*), and, unlike those Stickies, cannot contain images.

Stocks

Pulls current stock information from Quote.com's web services, providing you with a 20-minute-delayed ticker. To add a stock symbol for this Widget to track, click on the info icon ("i") in the lower-right corner.

Tile Game

Scrambles up a picture of a Leopard; it's your job to move the individual tiles around to put the picture back in its original state. To play this game, click one of the tiles to shuffle the tiles of the puzzle, click again to stop the tiles from shuffling, and then click a tile next to the empty space to move that tile into the empty space. Repeat until you put the puzzle back together again.

Translation

Translates words and phrases. Need to find out how to say "Where is the bathroom?" in Spanish? Look no further than the Translator Widget. Just type in the word (or words) you want to search for, then select the From and To languages from the pop-up menus. The translation instantly appears in the To field.

Unit Converter

Quickly converts various units of measure from one to another. This multifunction Widget includes a pop-up menu that lets you select Area, Energy, Temperature, Time, Length, Weight, Speed, Pressure, Power, or Volume. Each type lets you select From and To conversion types, so feel free to play around with these. For example, if you've ever wondered how many seconds there are in a year, you can find the answer here.

Weather

Uses information it gathers from AccuWeather.com's web services to provide you with up-to-date weather information for most major cities around the world.

Web Clip

This Widget provides you with a quick link that, when clicked, launches Safari so you can create your own Web Clippings. Web Clippings are new to Mac OS X Leopard, and they let you create a Widget from any portion of a web site.

World Clock

Tells you what time it is where you live, or, if you're using additional Clock Widgets, tells you the time elsewhere in the world. Between the hours of 6 a.m. and 6 p.m., the face is white, while between 6 p.m. and 6 a.m., the face is set to black. This is a quick way for you to tell if it's daytime or nighttime in the place for which the clock is set.

Now that you know what's available to you—Widget-wise— it's time to see how these things work.

Finding More Widgets

It won't take long before you're addicted to the Dashboard. You'll find lots of great uses for it, such as relying on the Dashboard's Clock Widget to get your time instead of taking up valuable space in the menu bar with the clock menu extra. But what if you want more? Where can you turn to find more Widgets?

If you look ahead at Figure 3-30, you'll notice another button, labeled "More Widgets," off to the right, just above the Dashboard's dock. When you click this button, you're taken to Apple's own Dashboard web site, located at *http:// www.apple.com/macosx/dashboard*. There you'll not only find more Widgets you can download and install on your Mac (save them to *~/Library/Widgets*), but you'll also find tutorials on how to build your own Dashboard Widget.

And if you're a whiz at web design, you can employ your own HTML, CSS, and JavaScript skills to build your own Dashboard Widget. To find out more information about building and designing Dashboard Widgets, take a read through Apple's Dashboard documentation, located at *http:// developer.apple.com*.

Viewing the Dashboard

There are three ways you can bring Dashboard Widgets into view:

- Click on the Dashboard's icon in the Dock
- Press the F12 key (Figure 3-29)
- Move your mouse to the Dashboard's Hot Corner (if you've set that up in System Preferences → Dashboard & Exposé → Dashboard → Hot Corners)

When you do, any previously running Dashboard Widgets come into view.

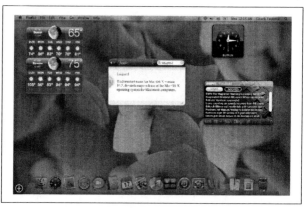

Figure 3-29. When you hit the F12 key, Dashboard Widgets pop into view, giving you quick access to the information or services they provide

As previously mentioned, there are only a couple of keyboard shortcuts you can use to get at the Dashboard. Table 3-6 has a complete list of them.

Table 3-6. The Dashboard's keyboard shortcuts

Key command	Description
F12 (or Fn-F12 with laptops)	Brings the Dashboard into view; hit this key again, and the Dashboard goes away.
Shift-F12 (or Shift-Fn-F12 with laptops)	Similar to using F12, except the Shift key brings the Dashboard into/out of view slowly (very slowly).

If you look closely at Figure 3-29, you'll notice a little circle with a plus sign (+) inside it at your display's lower-left corner. When you click this icon, your screen changes as Mac OS X Leopard's full Dashboard pops into view along the bottom as its own "dock" (as shown in Figure 3-30).

On either side of the Dashboard's dock, you'll see little arrows pointing left and right, respectively. This lets you

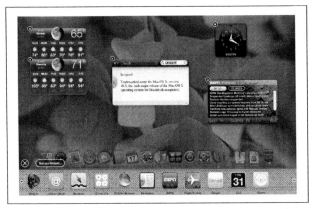

Figure 3-30. The Dashboard's dock gives you quick access to other Widgets installed on your Mac

know that there are more Widgets to view and use. Just click on one of these "scroller" arrows, and a new set of Widgets appears.

To use one of the other Widgets, just click the one you need to pop it into view, or click and drag the Widget's icon from the Dashboard's dock. This lets you drag the Widget to a screen location of your choice. To close a Widget (make it slip back down into the Dashboard's dock), just move your mouse over the Widget and hold down the Option key, and a circled × appears in the upper-left corner of the Widget. Click this ×, and the Widget goes away.

Managing and Installing Widgets

If you look closely at Figure 3-30, next to the circled × above the Dashboard's dock, you'll see a button that says Manage Widgets. When you click that, a special Widget appears (shown in Figure 3-31) that lets you manage the Widgets installed on your Mac.

Figure 3-31. The Widget Manager lets you manage the Widgets on your Mac

Using the Widget Manager, you can sort the list of Widgets by name or by the date they were installed, scroll through a list of the Widgets installed on your Mac, and even enable or disable Widgets using the checkboxes on the left. If you've installed any third-party Widgets on your Mac, you will see a red circle with a minus (–) sign to the right of the Widget's name. Clicking that red minus sign deletes that Widget from your Mac. This makes it incredibly easy to get rid of Widgets you aren't using anymore.

If you click on the More Widgets button at the bottom of the Widget Manager, you are taken to Apple's Dashboard Widget page using your default web browser. Here, you will find tons of Widgets you can install on your Mac (just don't get carried away and install all of them).

When you find a Widget on Apple's site that you would like to install, click the Download button, and the Widget is downloaded to your Mac. For example, say you're a cartoon fanatic and you need to search the Big Cartoon Database regularly (yes, it exists! *http://www.bcbd.com*). So, you find the Widget and download it from Apple's site, but before it gets installed, you see an alert dialog, as shown in Figure 3-32.

Figure 3-32. Just to be safe, the system asks you whether you want to install a Widget

If you click install, you're taken to the Dashboard, where you'll see the Widget you've downloaded in a white box, with options to either Keep or Delete the Widget, as shown in Figure 3-33. If you click Delete, the Widget you downloaded is moved to the Trash. If you click Keep, the Widget is installed in your *~/Library/Widgets* folder.

Now you can search the Big Cartoon Database to your heart's content. Me? I'm off to find out more about Screwball Squirrel's deep, dark past of tormenting other squirrels.

Widget Preferences

One of the cool things about Dashboard Widgets is that you can have multiple "versions" of the same Widget open at a time, just as you can have more than one Finder or Word document window open at any time. For example, let's say you're using the Weather Widget to monitor the six-day weather forecast where you live, but you also want to see

Figure 3-33. Here, you get to preview the Widget, and then decide whether to Delete or Keep it

what the weather is going to be like where your friend Scott is, in Chicago. You could always change the Widget's preferences to view the weather for Chicago and then change it back to your own city, but that just seems silly.

Instead, you can click again on the Weather Widget's icon in the Dashboard's dock to pop open another Widget. To change the preferences for that Widget so it tracks the weather in Chicago, move your mouse to the lower-right corner of the Weather Widget's window. You'll see a little "i" (information) icon appear; click this. The Widget "flips" over, revealing a field where you can set that window's preferences. You can either type in the city and state, or enter the zip code for the Widget, as shown in Figure 3-34.

Now when you press the F12 key to bring the Dashboard to the front, you'll see the weather report for both cities in two separate Weather Widgets, as shown in Figure 3-35.

Figure 3-34. To select another location in the Weather Widget's preferences, just type in the city and state, or the zip code, and click Done

Spotlight

One of the biggest innovations to hit Mac OS X has been Spotlight, and with Leopard, things have only gotten better. Spotlight combs through each and every file on your computer and creates an index not only of the filenames, but also of *every single word inside the files,* including words it finds tucked deep inside PDF files.

Figure 3-35. Same Widget, two different weather reports

Immediately after you install Mac OS X Leopard, whenever you log in to your account, and whenever you add,
change, or delete a file on your system, Spotlight jumps
into action and collects information known as *metadata*
about each and every file. And, if you've attached an external FireWire drive to your Mac, Spotlight indexes all of the
information on that drive as well.

TIP

You can opt to have Spotlight exclude certain files, folders,
or even data on external drives, from indexing. To configure this, go to System Preferences → Spotlight → Privacy,
and click the Add (+) button to add an item to the list of
things to exclude from Spotlight indexing. For example,
one item you might want to exclude is Mail's Junk Mail
box, which is located in *~/Library/Mail/Mailboxes*.

The metadata collected by Spotlight includes information about the file—the date it was created or changed, where it's located in the filesystem, etc.—as well as information about the words Spotlight finds inside the file. This makes Spotlight truly amazing, because you can do keyword searches and get results for any type of file found on your system.

TIP

Spotlight does not collect metadata for Unix files found at the system level; it only indexes files you access through the Aqua interface. If you're a Unix-head and you know what somebody means when they refer to "et-cee files" (files stored in the /etc directory), then you probably already know how to search through files using *find*, *locate*, or *grep*.

Now that you know what Spotlight is and a little about how it works, let's put it into action and *find* something.

Searching with Spotlight

To search with Spotlight, you can either click on the little magnifying glass icon, located at the far-right edge of the menu bar, or you can hit ⌘-Space to pop open Spotlight's Search field, as shown in Figure 3-36. Best of all, you can use that keyboard shortcut from within any application, which makes it really easy for you to search for something without having to switch over to the Finder.

Figure 3-36. Spotlight's Search field appears beneath the menu bar, attached to the Spotlight icon, as its own menu

To search for something, just type in a word or series of words (known as a *string*), as shown in Figure 3-37. Spotlight doesn't wait for you to finish typing to begin its metadata search; it starts searching as soon as you type the first character.

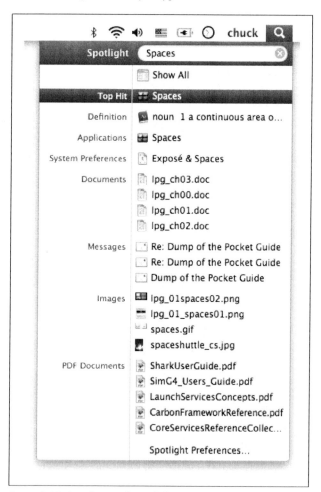

Figure 3-37. Searching with Spotlight

As you can see from Figure 3-37, Spotlight categorizes the search results in a menu beneath its Search field. This is very convenient because you don't have to sort through an alphabetical list of results; instead, you can see instantly whether the search term is in a Word or PDF file, or even buried deep within some iChat message.

Among Spotlight's search results, you'll notice three items that stand out—two at the top of the window and one at the bottom; everything in between relates to your search.

Show All

> If you select the Show All item, a Finder window opens, showing you all of the items that match your Spotlight search.

Top Hit

> Of all the files or folders on your Mac, Spotlight thinks the item shown here is the one for which you're looking. This may or may not be the correct item, though, so think twice before clicking on it.

TIP

To quickly select the Top Hit in Spotlight's results, press the ⌘ key.

Spotlight preferences…

> Click this item, and Spotlight's preferences panel opens in System Preferences. Use this window to configure Spotlight's search activities or even the keyboard shortcuts you use to access Spotlight's Search field or window (we'll get to that in a sec).

If you see the file you're looking for in Spotlight's search results, all you need to do to open the file is bring the mouse down and click the item once. However, if you can't find the file you're looking for and you know it should be there, you can choose the Show All option to open a Finder window (see Figure 3-38). This Finder window displays Spotlight's

search results and allows you to further tweak the search
results by adding more query items to your search.

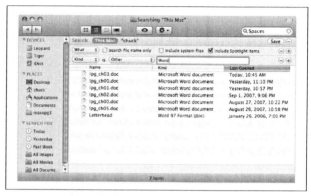

*Figure 3-38. The Finder lets you refine the search results, helping
you find the exact file you're looking for*

Spotlight's Preferences

As noted earlier, Spotlight has its own preference panel,
which is located in the System Preferences application (System Preferences → Spotlight). Use Spotlight's preference
panel to:

- Select the order in which Spotlight categorizes its search
  results. For example, if you know you'll mostly be
  searching for something within a document, you can
  click on the Documents item and drag it to the top of the
  list.
- Change the keyboard shortcut for accessing the Spotlight menu; by default, this is set to ⌘-Space.
- Change the keyboard shortcut for opening a Finder window to conduct Spotlight searches; by default, this is set
  to Option-⌘-Space.

You'll also notice that there's a Privacy tab in Spotlight's preference panel. Use this tab to choose items you don't want Spotlight to index and search through. For example, if you don't want Spotlight to display images in your iPhoto Library, click the Add button (+) and choose your Pictures folder on the sheet that appears.

Get Info and File Permissions

Get Info gives you access to all sorts of information about the files, directories, and applications on your system. To view the information for an item, click on its icon in the Finder and either go to File → Get Info or use the keyboard shortcut ⌘-I. The Get Info window has six different panes that each offer different kinds of information about the file. To reveal the content of one of these items, click on its disclosure triangle to expand the pane. The panes of the Get Info window include the following:

Spotlight Comments
> Here you'll find an empty text field in which you can type additional information about the file (such as "This is Chapter 3 for the Mac OS X Leopard Pocket Guide," or "This is for my blog"). The next time Spotlight indexes the files on your system, it picks up the information you entered in these fields and uses that as additional metadata for the file.

General
> This tells you the basics about the file, including its kind, its size, where it's located in the filesystem, and when it was created and last modified. If you are looking at the Info for a file, you will see two checkboxes in the General section: Stationery Pad and Locked. If you enable these options, the file can be used as a template or is made read-only, respectively.

TIP

If you use Get Info on an Application (such as Safari), you will see that the Stationery Pad checkbox is gone. However, if you are using an Intel Mac and the application is a Universal Binary, you will see an "Open using Rosetta" checkbox as an option.

When checked, this allows you to run an application as if it were built only for a PowerPC Mac using Rosetta. Unless you really need to test out the performance of an application under Rosetta, you should leave this unchecked, because that application might run slower and take up more CPU and memory space than it should.

More Info

For folders and hard drives (including partitions and disk images), the More Info box displays the date and time the item was last opened. For files, the same information is displayed; however, Word files display the author (or creator) of the file, and image files display information such as the image's dimensions (in pixels) and its color space (such as RGB, CMYK, or Gray for grayscale images).

Name & Extension

This displays a text box with the name of the file or directory.

Open with

This option is available only if you select a file (i.e., not a folder or an application). Here you can specify which application opens this file or all similar files.

Preview

Depending on the file type, you can preview the contents of the file here (this also works for playing sounds and QuickTime movies).

Sharing & Permissions
>   This displays the name of the owner and the name of the
>   group to which the file belongs. It also allows you to set
>   access privileges to that file for the Owner, Group, and
>   Others on the system.

The Get Info window for applications includes the General
Information, Name & Extension, and Sharing & Permissions options mentioned previously (although the Owner-
ship & Permissions options are disabled by default), as well
as one or both of the following options:

Languages
>   This shows the languages the application supports. The
>   languages are displayed with checkboxes next to them.
>   To make an application run faster, turn off the ones you
>   don't need by unchecking the box.

Plug-ins
>   If applicable, this lists the available plug-ins for the appli-
>   cation. For example, iMovie and iPhoto's Get Info win-
>   dows have a Plug-ins section.

TIP

Noticeably missing from a Mac OS X application's Get
Info window is the Memory option. Because memory for
applications is assigned dynamically by virtual memory,
you no longer have to specify how much memory an application requires.

CHAPTER 4

System Preferences

Before Mac OS X came along, you'd have to fumble through the Control Panels to set up your Mac, but now, Apple has made all these "panels" self-contained in the System Preferences application. When you want to set up your Mac just for you, System Preferences is the application you're looking for. To launch the System Preferences application, simply click on its icon in the Dock (it's the one that looks like a silver window with three gears inside), and the window shown in Figure 4-1 appears.

System Preferences is home to a series of preference panels you use for configuring your Mac. For example, if you wanted to select Mac OS X Leopard's new Word of the Day screensaver, you would launch System Preferences by clicking its icon in the Dock, and then click Desktop & Screen Saver. This opens the preference panel shown in Figure 4-2. It has two tabbed "panes," aptly named Desktop and Screen Saver. To change the settings for your screensaver, click the tab for the Screen Saver pane, then select a screensaver from the list on the lefthand side of the window.

As you may have noticed in Figure 4-1, the System Preferences are separated into four categories: Personal, Hardware, Internet & Network, and System. When you click one of the icons, the window changes to reflect that particular panel's settings. To go back to the main view, click the Show All button (View → Show All Preferences, or use the keyboard

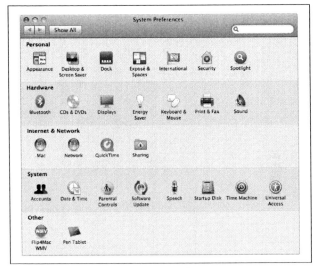

Figure 4-1. The System Preferences window

shortcut, ⌘-L). You can also select View → Organize Alphabetically; this menu option changes the view of the System Preferences window to that shown in Figure 4-3.

When you've completed setting your Mac's preferences, you can quit System Preferences by selecting System Preferences → Quit (⌘-Q), or by simply closing the System Preferences window using Window → Close (⌘-W).

NOTE

Some of the System Preferences panels require administrator privileges. If you attempt to change a setting and are asked for a password, try using the password you used to log in to the computer. If that doesn't work, contact your system administrator for assistance.

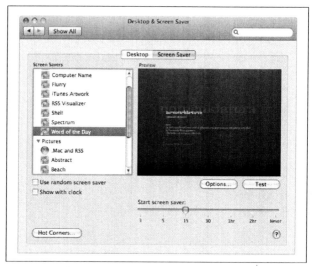

Figure 4-2. The Desktop & Screen Saver preference panel

Figure 4-3. The System Preferences, listed alphabetically

Searching for Preferences

If you take a close look at System Preferences' toolbar (along the top of the window), you'll notice a Search field. While the thought of having a Search field in System Preferences might seem odd, it really comes in handy for those times when you have an idea of what it is you want to do, but aren't quite sure which System Preferences panel will do the trick. When you find yourself stuck like that, the Search field quickly comes to the rescue.

To search within System Preferences, either click in the Search field in the toolbar, or use the standard Mac keyboard shortcut for "find," which is ⌘-F. For example, if you're a former Windows user who is new to the Mac, you might not be familiar with the Mac lingo. So, when you go to System Preferences and want to set a new desktop image, you might still be thinking of "wallpaper." To help find what you're looking for, start typing "wallpaper" in System Preferences' Search field, as shown in Figure 4-4.

In this case, since you're looking for "wallpaper," you'll see that "Desktop picture" shows up as one of the options in System Preferences' search results. To open this panel, simply move your mouse down and click on "Desktop picture." The circle of light (a spotlight—cute, huh?) flashes twice on the Desktop & Screen Saver panel, which opens it up in the window.

TIP

You can also use the arrow keys to highlight items in System Preferences' search results. This can be somewhat entertaining, as pressing the Down or Up arrow keys focuses the Spotlight on the corresponding panel, giving you a Christmas tree-like effect as the glow moves around the window. Go on, give it a try—you know you want to.

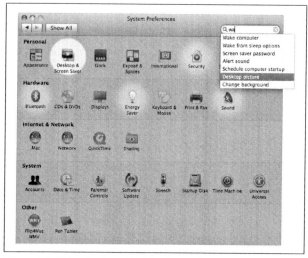

Figure 4-4. Using the Search field in Leopard's System Preferences lets you quickly find the right preference panel for configuring your Mac

System Preferences Overview

The next four sections provide an overview of the controls found in the System Preferences.

Personal

These items control the general look and feel of the Aqua interface.

Appearance

When selected, this panel lets you specify the colors used for buttons and menu items, the location of scrollbar arrows (top and bottom, or together), and how a click in the scrollbar is interpreted (scroll down one page or scroll to that location in the document). Here, you can specify the number of recent items to be remembered and listed in the → Recent Items menu for applications and documents, as well as determine which font-smoothing style and size is best for your type of display.

Dashboard & Exposé

This preference panel lets you configure the settings for Dashboard and Exposé's Hot Corners.

Desktop & Screen Saver

This panel has two panes, one you can use to set the background image for your desktop, and the other to select your screensaver. The Desktop pane lets you choose the pattern, image, or color of your desktop. If you click on the checkbox next to "Change picture" at the bottom of the window, the desktop picture changes automatically based on the timing you select in the pull-down menu.

The Screen Saver pane lets you select one of Mac OS X's default screensaver modules. Here, you can set the amount of time your system must be inactive before the screensaver kicks in, require a password to turn the screensaver off, and specify Hot Corners for enabling or disabling the screensaver. For example, you could set the upper-right corner of your display to start the screensaver and the lower-right corner to prevent the screensaver from turning on if your mouse is located there.

TIP

If you have a .Mac account, you can also choose from the .Mac Screen Effects or subscribe to another .Mac member's public slide show. To do this, click on the Configure button and enter the member's username (for example, *chuckdude*).

A new addition to the Screen Saver panel in Mac OS X Leopard is the ability to set the Display Style for how Pictures are displayed in Screen Saver mode. The three new options are Slideshow, Collage, and Mosaic, which you can specify by clicking one of the three buttons along the bottom of the Preview window, as shown in Figure 4-5.

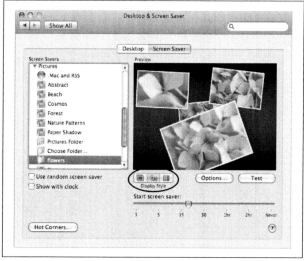

Figure 4-5. Leopard's new Display Style lets you specify how your photos are displayed when used as a screensaver

The new Mosaic screensaver creates a mosaic of one image using other images from your iPhoto Library.

TIP

You can only select the Mosaic Display Style if you have an iPhoto Library to choose images from.

Dock

This is one of the ways you can configure your Dock (another is by going to → Dock → Dock Preferences). See "The Dock" in Chapter 3 for more details.

International

This is used to set the languages supported by your system. The language you specify during the installation process will be the default. Also found here are controls to format the date, time, numbers, and currency, as well

---

as the keyboard layout to be used for a country and its language.

If you select more than one language in the tabbed Input Menu pane, a menu extra appears in the menu bar showing flags of the countries whose languages are supported on your system.

TIP

Earlier versions of Mac OS X let you use ⌘-Space to toggle between keyboard languages in the Input Menu. However, Leopard uses ⌘-Space to open and close Spotlight's Search field. If you want to set a keyboard shortcut for the Input Menu so you can switch from U.S. English to Canadian English (trust me, it's an option), use the Keyboard Shortcuts pane in the Keyboard & Mouse preference pane.

Security

Leopard's Security panel has undergone some revisions, bringing together the different panels that allow you to keep your Mac—and all the data on it—safe and secure. When you open the Security panel, you'll notice three tabs—General, FileVault, and Firewall (which used to be in the Sharing panel in earlier versions of Mac OS X):

General

The General pane lets you set basic security features for your Mac, including requiring a password to wake your Mac from Screen Saver or Sleep mode, and options to disable automatic login, to require a password to access each System Preferences panel, and to automatically log off if your account has been inactive for a specified amount of time. If you have a MacBook or MacBook Pro with an infrared remote, there's also an option to disable the IR sensor, which could make your Mac vulnerable to other X10 devices.

FileVault

> This tab lets you set up a FileVault for your Home folder by encrypting its contents. FileVault uses Kerberos authentication to encrypt and decrypt files automatically. To enable FileVault, you'll need to set the master password, and then click the "Turn on FileVault" button. After entering your login password (not the master password you've just set), you can turn on FileVault protection. All of the files in your Home folder are encrypted with your login password. This protects your files from being accessed by other users on your computer, or from someone who might boot your Mac into Target mode (see Table 2-1 in Chapter 2) with malicious intent. When FileVault finishes encrypting your files, you are required to log back in, after which you'll notice that the icon for your Home folder in the Finder has changed from a friendly-looking house to one that looks like an imposing metallic safe.

Firewall

> As noted earlier, the Firewall panel used to be located in the Sharing panel in earlier versions of Mac OS X. In Leopard, the Firewall settings have been simplified to make it easier for the average user to set up her firewall and protect her Mac.

Spotlight

> This panel gives you added control when you're using Spotlight. Use the Search Results pane to configure the order in which Spotlight displays its results. You can uncheck items you don't want displayed in the search results, or you can drag them around in the list. For example, if you want the contacts in your Address Book to appear first, simply click on Contacts and drag it to the top of the list; the other items move down in the chain. If there are any folders or disks you don't want Spotlight to index (such as Mail's Junk mailbox), use the Privacy pane.

The two checkboxes at the bottom (and their corresponding pop-up menus) let you configure the keyboard shortcuts used to open Spotlight's Search field in the menu bar (set to ⌘-Space by default) as well as the Spotlight window (set to Option-⌘-Space by default).

Hardware

These panels are used to control the settings for the devices connected to your computer:

Bluetooth
> This panel allows you to configure the settings for using Bluetooth to pair your Mac with Bluetooth devices, such as a mouse, keyboard, mobile phone (such as the iPhone), printer, headset, or some other Bluetooth device. This item appears only if you have a Bluetooth-enabled Mac (such as the MacBook Pro, MacBook, iMac, or Mac mini), or if you are using a USB dongle that adds Bluetooth capabilities to an older Mac.

CDs & DVDs
> The items in the CDs & DVDs panel all share the same basic interface: a pull-down menu that lets you choose what the Mac does when it mounts various kinds of discs. You can choose to have it simply open the new media volume as a Finder window, launch an appropriate application (such as iTunes for music CDs and Disk Utility for blank discs), run a script, or prompt you to take some other action.

Displays
> This panel lets you set your monitor's resolution and color depth (256, thousands, or millions of colors). It also has an option to include a monitor menu extra in the menu bar, as well as a slider control to set your monitor's brightness. If you have more than one monitor connected to your system, clicking on the Detect Displays button allows you to specify settings for each display.

TIP

If you use a CRT display, the Displays panel also offers a Rotate pop-up menu, which lets you rotate the display (clockwise) 90 degrees at a time. For example, select 180 and watch your display flip upside-down. Of course, this makes it a little more difficult to use your mouse, but it sure looks goofy. (The Rotate feature is not available on laptop computers, such as the MacBook or MacBook Pro.)

Energy Saver

This panel is used to set the autosleep settings for your computer. Here, you can specify the amount of time your system must be idle before Energy Saver puts your monitor, hard drive, or the entire system to sleep.

PowerBook and iBook users will also see two pull-down menus at the top of this panel. The first pull-down menu, Settings for, gives you options for controlling the Energy Saver settings for when you're plugged in (Power Adapter) or when you're operating on battery (Battery). The second, Optimization, lets you either select from four preset options or specify custom settings.

Ink

This item appears only if you have a graphics tablet (such as a Wacom tablet) connected to your system. Ink controls how handwritten text is handled in InkPad. The Gestures tab includes pen strokes for invoking commands such as Undo, Cut, Copy, Paste, insert a space or carriage return (Vertical Space), and more.

Keyboard & Mouse

This panel contains the following four panes:

Keyboard

This pane controls the repeat rate, or the rate at which a key repeats when you depress it and hold it down. You can specify the speed of the repeat (from slow to fast) and the delay between the time the key is first depressed until the repeat option kicks in (from long to short). If you select the Off option for Delay Until Repeat, the repeat feature will be disabled entirely.

Mouse (or Trackpad, if you have a MacBook Pro or MacBook)

This pane lets you specify the mouse's Tracking Speed as well as the delay between double-clicks. If you are using an MacBook or MacBook Pro, the Mouse preferences panel will have an additional section for setting the controls for your Trackpad.

One cool feature to try out if you have a MacBook or MacBook Pro is the "Zoom while holding" option, which lets you specify a special key to invoke the feature. By default, this is set to the Control key. If you hold down the Control key and place two fingers on the trackpad, you can quickly zoom in or out by sliding your fingers up or down. This is a great shortcut to remember when you're giving a presentation and someone asks you to zoom in on something.

Bluetooth

This pane lets you configure the settings for Apple's Bluetooth keyboard and mouse, if you have them. The Mouse and Keyboard sections have indicators to show the battery level for each device.

Keyboard Shortcuts

This pane lists the various keyboard shortcuts you can use on your Mac. You can also add, remove, or change the shortcuts to suit your needs.

At the bottom of this window are two radio buttons for controlling Full Keyboard Access, one of the many accessibility features built into Mac OS X Leopard. Full Keyboard Access is always on in Mac OS X Leopard, which means anyone can use his keyboard to perform all the functions of the mouse, without ever having to use the mouse—you use the keys on your keyboard instead. Full Keyboard Access lets you use the Tab key to set the keyboard focus to either "Text boxes and lists only" or "All controls" (the default setting). For example, with "Text boxes and lists only" selected, you use the Tab key to move among the Full Keyboard Access key combinations listed in Table 4-1.

Table 4-1. Full Keyboard Access's key combinations

Function keys	Description
Control-F1	Enable/disable keyboard access.
Control-F2	Control the menu bar.
Control-F3	Control the Dock.
Control-F4	Activate the window or the first window behind it.
Control-F5	Control an application's toolbar.
Control-F6	Control an application's utility window (or palette).
Control-F7	Highlight either text input fields and lists, or any window control (used for windows and dialogs).
Control-F8	Move the focus to the status menus at the right side of the menu bar.
Esc	Return control to the mouse, disabling the Control-Fx key combination.
Spacebar	Perform the function of a mouse click.

TIP

If you are using a MacBook or MacBook Pro, you need to use Control plus the fn key, along with the Function or Letter key for keyboard access, to perform the commands in Table 4-1; for example, Control-*fn*-F2 to access menus, or Control-*fn*-F3 to switch to the Dock. The *fn* key is at the bottom-left corner of your keyboard, to the left of the Control key (and below the Shift key).

Print & Fax

This panel is used to configure printers and set up your Mac to accept faxes. To add a printer or fax to your Mac, simply click the Add (+) button, and in the window that appears, select the item you wish to add to your Mac from the window's toolbar. From the Faxing pane, you can opt to have incoming faxes sent directly to your default printer.

Sound

This panel offers three panes: one for configuring the Sound Effects for Alert sounds, one for sound Output (e.g., speakers), and one for sound Input (e.g., microphone). The Sound Effects pane has an option for including a volume control slider in the menu bar.

Internet & Network

The following panels are used to control your Mac's settings for connecting to other computers:

.Mac

This panel has four tabbed panes: Account, Sync, iDisk, and Back To My Mac, which allow you to configure the settings for your .Mac account, see how much space is available on your iDisk, or set up Leopard's .Mac Sync features.

The Back To My Mac feature, new to Leopard, lets you access files and services on your Mac from another Mac that has Back To My Mac enabled. Of course, those other Macs must be yours for this to work, but Back To My Mac opens the door for letting you access files on your Mac at home from your Mac at work.

Network

This panel lets you configure your settings for AirPort, Ethernet, Bluetooth, and FireWire networking, including enabling/disabling AppleTalk. For details on how to configure these settings, see Chapter 6.

QuickTime

This panel lets you configure QuickTime's settings for playing back movies and music. If you've purchased a license for QuickTime Pro, enter the registration number in the Registration Code field so you'll have full access to QuickTime's features.

Sharing

This panel lets you set the name of your computer and your Bonjour name. The lower portion of the Sharing panel lets you enable and disable different services, such as File Sharing, Screen Sharing, and Printer Sharing (among others). To enable a service, simply click the On checkbox next to a service, and then configure its settings to the right.

System

The items in the System panel allow you to configure a variety of settings for your computer:

Accounts

As the name implies, this panel is used to add and remove users, and to make changes to their identities and passwords.

TIP

If you have administrator privileges, you can also specify Parental Controls for a non-administrator's account for doing things such as removing items from the Dock, using the System Preferences, changing passwords, burning CDs or DVDs, and even restricting which applications and utilities are available to the user. For more information, see the section "Parental Controls" in Chapter 2.

Date & Time

This panel is used to set the date, time, and time zone for your system, specify a network time server, and specify how (or whether) the date and time appear in the menu bar.

WARNING

Want more space in your menu bar? Turn off the menu bar clock by unchecking the box next to "Show the date and time" in the Date & Time → Clock preference pane in System Preferences. Since you have the Dashboard at your disposal, whenever you need to know what time it is, just hit F12, look at the Dashboard's World Clock Widget, and then hit F12 again to make the clock (and all the other Widgets you have open) go away.

Parental Controls

One of the greatest improvements made to System Preferences in Leopard is the new suite of Parental Controls, which lets a system administrator (or parent) control how other users can use the system. To better protect your children from unsavory types on the Internet, you can control whom they can Instant Message (IM) with, whom they can email, and even which web sites they can visit using Safari. You can also protect them from any profane words in the Dictionary.

Furthermore, parents can restrict the hours their children can use the Mac. For example, you can set the number of hours your kids may use the Mac on weekdays and weekends, and even set limits that restrict them from using the Mac after and before a certain hour. For example, you can cut off their access to the computer after 9 p.m., and set it so they can't use the Mac before 8 a.m. when you're likely to be awake.

Software Update

This panel is used to check for updates to your Mac OS X system and other Apple applications, such as the iLife or iWork applications. You can check for updates manually (i.e., when you want to, or when you learn of an available update) or automatically (daily, weekly, or monthly). When an update is found, you are prompted to specify which updates will be downloaded and installed on your system.

If you enable the "Download important updates in the background" checkbox, Software Update automatically downloads and installs important updates, such as Security Updates.

Speech

This panel is used to turn on and configure speech recognition, specify a default voice for applications that speak text, and specify whether items in the user interface (such as alert messages or the text in menus) will be spoken.

Startup Disk

This panel is used to specify the hard drive or partition that your Mac uses to boot into Mac OS X. With Leopard, you can also specify a Network Startup disk if your computer is configured or set up via NetBoot from Mac OS X Server. Leopard's Startup Disk panel also features a Target Disk Mode button, which, when clicked, restarts your Mac and allows you to mount its hard drive as a FireWire drive on another Mac.

Time Machine

This panel lets you turn Time Machine on or off, and allows you to specify a drive that you can back up your system to.

Universal Access

This panel provides support for people with disabilities. It features two panes for people who have problems seeing or hearing, and two more panes for those who find it difficult to use a keyboard or mouse. The Universal Access panel also lets you turn VoiceOver on or off, and includes a button that opens the VoiceOver Utility (*/Applications/Utilities*).

TIP

One thing you'll notice quickly is that all the text labels for the user interface elements in the Universal Access panel are spoken using the voice you've specified in the Speech panel.

To quit the System Preferences application, you can use either ⌘-Q or ⌘-W. (Yes, closing the System Preferences window also quits the application.)

CHAPTER 5

Applications and Utilities

What good is a computer without programs to run on it?
Apple has included a set of native applications and utilities
for Mac OS X, including the famous suite of iApps (iCal,
iChat, iSync, and iTunes), along with a bunch of uilities to
help you monitor and set up additional gear for your Mac.

There are applications for things such as viewing and printing PostScript and PDF files, basic word processing, sending
and receiving email, and creating movies, as well as utilities
to help you manage your system.

Use the Finder to locate the applications (*/Applications*) and
utilities (*/Applications/Utilities*) on your system. You can
quickly go to the Applications folder either by clicking on the
Applications icon in the Sidebar or by using the Shift-⌘-A
keyboard shortcut. If you want to be able to get to the Utilities folder quickly, you might consider dragging the Utilities
folder icon to the Finder's Sidebar, or instead using its keyboard shortcut, Shift-⌘-U.

Applications

Following is a list of the programs found in the Applications
directory:

Address Book

This is a database program you can use to store contact information for your friends and colleagues.

AppleScript

This folder contains all the tools necessary for writing AppleScripts. AppleScript is an "English-like" scripting language native to the Mac, which you can use to help automate tasks, such as renaming a bunch of files or applying a Photoshop filter to a group of graphics you need for your web site. Inside the AppleScript folder you'll find the following items:

AppleScript Utility

This little program lets you choose a script editor (which is set to Mac OS X's Script Editor by default), turn on GUI scripting (requires an administrator's password), and set up Folder Actions. It also offers an option for turning on the Script Menu for the menu bar.

Folder Actions Setup

This program lets you turn on Folder Actions and, once they're enabled, allows you to specify and track folders that have a Folder Action script applied to them.

Script Editor

The Script Editor is the application with which you'll create your AppleScripts.

You'll also see an alias to the Example Scripts folder (you'll know it's an alias because the folder icon has a little arrow on it), which is located in the main Library folder on your hard drive (Macintosh HD → Library).

Automator

Automator is the killer app for users who need to automate processes, such as renaming a bunch of files in a folder, or converting images for your web site from PNGs to JPEGs. To use Automator, first select the application you want to control, then find an Action you want it to perform and drag that to the Workflow area. Need the Finder to hand off a process to Preview or iPhoto? No problem—there are Actions for those applications, too.

TIP

Apple created an Automator web site for downloading and sharing Automator Actions. You can access this web site quickly by selecting "Display Automator Website" from Automator's application menu or by pointing your web browser to *http://www.apple.com/macosx/features/ automator*.

Calculator

The Calculator is a fully functional scientific calculator. Calculator also has a Paper Tape sheet that allows you to view the math functions, which you can then copy and paste into another document window.

Chess

The Chess program is based on GNU Chess. Apple has packaged this Unix-based chess game with a Cocoa interface and 3D game pieces.

Dashboard

Like the Finder, the Dashboard application is always running on your Mac. The Dashboard offers a set of "Widgets" that you can use to check the time or weather, see how your stock portfolio is doing, or check your friend's flight status, to name a few. See "The Dashboard" in Chapter 3 for an overview of the Dashboard Widgets that come with Mac OS X Leopard.

Dictionary

This application is very similar to the Dashboard's Dictionary Widget, mentioned in the section "The Dashboard" in Chapter 3. Use Dictionary to find the correct spelling and/or definition of a word that's stumping you. The Dictionary also features a built-in thesaurus, so you can look up alternatives for a word you might be overusing.

DVD Player

You can use this application to view DVD movies on your Mac. If your hardware natively supports DVD playback, the DVD Player is installed.

Exposé

Exposé lets you quickly scoot application windows out of the way, or separate and cycle through them, so you can quickly get at the application you need or at something on your Desktop. Exposé is covered in greater detail in Chapter 4.

Font Book

The Font Book application offers an intuitive way to preview the fonts on your Mac, as well as the ability to create font collections.

Front Row

Front Row provides an interface that's entirely different from the normal Mac OS X interface. When you launch Front Row (either by double-clicking its application icon or by using ⌘-Esc), the standard Mac interface disappears, and Front Row's graphic-heavy interface comes to the "front" of your Mac.

Front Row provides an interface for watching movies or TV shows, listening to Music or Podcasts in your iTunes collection, and viewing photos in your iPhoto Library. Mainly used with Apple TV, Front Row is available on all new Macs with Leopard.

iCal

For Leopard, iCal has received a thorough revamp of the application. iCal and Mail now share a common bond, in that meeting invitations received in Mail can be automatically added as iCal events. iCal is a calendaring application (similar to Entourage, if you're a Windows convert) that allows you to manage and publish your calendar to any CalDAV-enabled server (including your .Mac account). You can also subscribe to other calendars (such as a listing of holidays, the schedule for your favorite sports team, or another user's calendar).

iChat

iChat allows you to chat with other .Mac members, and AOL Instant Messenger (AIM) and Jabber users. iChat also supports messaging via Bonjour for dynamically finding iChat users on your local network. The new version of iChat for Leopard adds a picture-taker control so you can take your picture and apply different visual effects to your image (or the background). It's worth noting that some of these effects require a heftier graphics card in your Mac, so some users won't get full access to all the graphics goodies.

Another cool feature added to iChat in Leopard is the ability to share your screen with another Mac user while you're chatting. For example, say that your friend Gus is having trouble figuring out where something is on his Mac. If you're both running Mac OS X Leopard, Gus can share his screen with you, which gives you control of his Mac so you can open Finder windows, run or quit applications, etc., to help him out.

Also new to iChat is the ability to group all of your chat windows into one single chat window with tabs. To enable this feature, open iChat's preferences (⌘-,), click the Messages icon at the top, and then turn on the checkbox next to "Collect chats into a single window." Now if you're chatting with more than one person, you will see a tab bar along the left side of the window showing you who you're chatting with. To switch between chat sessions, either click on the tab for the person you want to chat with, or use Shift-⌘-{ or Shift-⌘-} to go up or down in the list. This is a great feature, as it reduces the number of windows you might have open—that is, of course, if you do a lot of chatting.

Image Capture

This program can be used to download pictures and video from a digital camera to your Mac. You can share input devices such as digital cameras and scanners attached to your Mac with other users on a network. To enable device sharing, go to Image Capture → Devices → Browse Devices → select a device, and then click the Sharing button.

iSync

iSync can be used to synchronize data—contact information from your Address Book, your iCal calendars, and Safari's bookmarks—from your computer to another device such as a cellular phone (including the iPhone), PDA, iPod, or another computer.

NOTE

As of Mac OS X Leopard, iSync no longer works for synchronizing your data to your .Mac account. Instead, you'll need to use the .Mac preference panel's Sync pane (System Preferences → .Mac → Sync).

---

iTunes

iTunes can be used to play CDs, listen to Internet radio stations, import (rip) music from CDs, burn CDs from music you've collected, and store and play MP3 files. If you have an iPod, you can use iTunes to synchronize your MP3 music files.

iTunes also serves as the virtual storefront for the iTunes Music Store (ITMS). If you have an Apple account, you can use the ITMS to purchase AAC-encoded music files for $.99 each. For more information about the iTunes Music Store, visit Apple's page at *http://www.apple.com/music/store*.

Mail

Mail is the standard email application that ships with Mac OS X. Mail received another overhaul for Leopard, giving it new features such as:

- Notes help you to be more productive, by providing you with a space where you can quickly type in notes to yourself. Notes show up on the left side of Mail's window, under the Reminders heading.

- To Dos, like Notes, help you schedule things that you need to do. For example, if you know you want to take your bike to the shop for a tune-up while you're away on vacation, you can set up a To Do and set an alarm to the item, and it will appear in the left side of Mail's window under the Reminders heading. To Dos also automatically appear in iCal, too.

- In the New message window (which you get with ⌘-N), you'll see two new buttons in the toolbar: Photo Browser and Stationery:

— Clicking the Photo Browser button gives you access to all of the photos in your iPhoto Library as well as any you've taken with Photo Booth. Simply drag an image into the new message window to attach the image to the message.

— Stationery lets you apply a graphical page template to your email message so you can send customized messages such as invites, thank-you notes, and even vacation reports that include pictures from your iPhoto Library. To apply an image to one of the Stationery templates, select a template, open the Photo Browser, and then drag and drop images into the Stationery—it's that simple.

Mail also lets you take advantage of Smart Folders, which you can use to help sort and sift your email for you, similar to having your own Cliff Claven inside your computer. What's more, Spotlight indexes all your email messages, which means they're all searchable.

Photo Booth

Photo Booth lets you use your Mac's iSight camera to take snapshots of you (and anyone in front of your Mac's screen). Photo Booth not only lets you take still images, but you can also use it to record video.

The coolest part about Photo Booth is that you can apply different effects to your image before you take the shot. For example, you can switch from color to black and white or sepia, use a Core Image filter to twist and distort your image, or apply a background image (such as the Eiffel Tower) to the shot. You will also see the Effects browser show up in applications such as iChat and even the System Preferences' Accounts pane.

Preview

Preview lets you open (and export) files that have been saved in a variety of image formats, including PICT, GIF, JPEG, and TIFF, and can be used to view raw PostScript files. It can also be used to open, view, and search through PDF files. Preview also lets you Annotate PDF files, copy selections from an image, and much more.

QuickTime Player

This is used for playing QuickTime movies as well as for listening to QuickTime streaming audio and video. QuickTime Player supports the H.264 encoding scheme, which allows video to seamlessly scale from high-definition quality down to video you can watch on your cell phone.

Safari

Safari is a fast, Cocoa-based web browser that ships with Mac OS X. If you want to use another browser as the default, you can change this in Safari's preferences (Safari → Preferences → General → Default Web Browser).

Safari also has a built-in RSS reader, which lets you check RSS feeds from various web sites so you can keep up-to-date with the latest news from your favorite sites.

Spaces

As mentioned in Chapter 1, Spaces adds an entirely new dimension to your Mac by giving you additional, virtual, desktop spaces for you to work within. For more information on how to use Spaces, see Chapter 1.

Stickies

Stickies is a simple application that lets you create sticky notes on your screen. Similar to the notes you stick to your desk or computer, Stickies can be used to store important notes and reminders.

System Preferences

The System Preferences application is described extensively in Chapter 4 and is addressed throughout this book.

TextEdit

TextEdit is the default application for creating text and rich text documents on Mac OS X. TextEdit includes a ruler bar with text-formatting buttons for changing the alignment, leading, and indentation of text. By default, TextEdit documents are saved in rich text format (*.rtf* or *.rtfd*), but you can also save documents as plain text (*.txt*) via the Format → Make Plain Text menu option. TextEdit replaces the SimpleText application from earlier versions of the Mac OS.

Best of all, TextEdit can open Word files (*.doc*), making it possible for you to read, print, and edit files created with Microsoft Word even if you don't have Microsoft Office installed on your Mac. However, TextEdit's compatibility with Word is limited; for example, TextEdit can't interpret Word files that use change tracking.

Time Machine

Time Machine provides a method for backing up the data on your Mac on a regular basis. Configured using the Time Machine preferences panel (see Chapter 1), once your system has been backed up, Time Machine can help you quickly locate and recover lost files, or even revert to an older version of a file from a day or two ago.

The very last item you'll see in the Applications folder is the Utilities folder, which leads us to the next section.

Utilities

The tools found in the Utilities folder can be used to help you manage your Mac:

Activity Monitor

The Activity Monitor lets you view the processes running on your system and provides a way for you to see the CPU load, how memory is allocated, and disk activity, disk usage, and network activity. If you click on a process name, you can see additional information about that process, or you can cancel (*kill*, in Unix-speak) by highlighting a process and choosing Process → Quit (Option-⌘-Q).

AirPort Utility

This utility is used to set up and administer AirPort Base Stations.

Audio MIDI Setup

This utility is used to add, set up, and configure Musical Instrument Digital Interface (MIDI) devices connected to your Mac. If you use GarageBand, you'll find the Audio MIDI Setup utility to be quite helpful in connecting your keyboard, guitar, or other musical device to your Mac.

Bluetooth File Exchange

This utility allows you to exchange files with other Bluetooth-enabled devices, such as cellular phones, PDAs, and other computers. To send a file, launch this utility and then drag a file from the Finder to the Bluetooth File Exchange icon in the Dock. A window appears asking you to select a recipient (or recipients) for the file.

Boot Camp Assistant

If you have one of the Intel-based Macs (such as a MacBook or an iMac), you can use the Boot Camp Assistant to assist you with installing Microsoft Windows XP or Vista on your Mac. When run, the Boot Camp Assistant partitions your Mac's hard drive and walks you through the process of installing the Windows operating system on the newly created disk partition. Once Windows is installed, you can boot directly into Windows by holding down the Option key at startup, or by switching to the Windows partition in the Startup Disk preference panel (System Preferences → Startup Disk).

ColorSync Utility

This utility has four main functions. By pressing the Profile First Aid icon, you can use it to verify and repair your ColorSync settings. The Profiles icon keeps track of the ColorSync profiles for your system, and the Devices icon lets you see which ColorSync devices are connected as well as the name and location of the current profile. The Filters icon lets you apply filters to selected items within a PDF document.

Console

The Console is used primarily to log the interactions between applications on your system and between those applications and the operating system itself. The Console gives you quick and easy access to system and crash logs via the Logs icon in its toolbar. The crash log created by the Console application can be used by developers to help debug their applications and should be supplied to Apple if you come across a bug in Mac OS X.

DigitalColor Meter

This small application lets you view and copy the color settings of any pixel on your screen.

Directory Utility

This utility controls access for Mac OS X systems to Directory Services such as NetInfo, LDAP, Active Directory, and BSD flat files, as well as Discovery Services such as AppleTalk, Bonjour, SLP, and SMB.

Directory

This utility gives you access to shared information about people, groups, locations, and resources within your organization. You can use Directory to share contacts, set up group services, and manage your own contact information. The information you share is located on a directory server provided by your organization.

Directory takes advantage of several Mac OS X applications. You can create shared contacts from your Address Book entries, click email addresses to send email using Mail, click chat names to chat with people in iChat, or load group web services in Safari.

Disk Utility

This utility lets you create disk images (*.dmg*) for batching and sending files (including folders and applications) from one Mac user to another. It can also be used to repair a damaged hard drive, erase rewriteable media such as CD-RWs, and initialize and partition new drives.

TIP

If you have unmounted an external FireWire drive but haven't unplugged it from your Mac, you can use Disk Utility to mount it again. Simply select the drive in the left pane and click the Mount button in the toolbar.

Grab

This utility can be used to take screenshots of your system. Two of its most useful features include the ability to select the pointer (or no pointer at all) to be displayed in the screenshot, and the ability to start a 10-second timer before the screenshot is taken to give you the necessary time to set up the shot.

Grapher

This application can be used to plot complex math equations.

Java

The following utilities can be found in the Java directory:

Input Method Hotkey

This utility allows you to set a hotkey that, when pressed while running a Java application, displays a pop-up menu that lets you select an input method.

Java Preferences

This controls Java settings when Java runs in a browser. This utility lets you specify browser support for J2SE 1.4.2 or J2SE 5.0.

Java Web Start

Java Web Start (JWS) can be used to download and run Java applications.

Keychain Access

This utility can be used to create and manage your passwords for accessing secure web and FTP sites, networked filesystems, and other items such as password-encoded files. You can also use Keychain Access to create secure, encrypted notes that can be read only by using this utility.

Migration Assistant

This utility helps you move your data from an existing Mac or Windows computer to your Mac OS X System.

Network Utility

This utility is a graphical frontend to a standard set of Unix tools such as *netstat*, *ping*, *lookup*, *traceroute*, *whois*, and *finger*. It also lets you view specific information about your network connection, view stats about your AppleTalk connections, and scan the available ports for a particular domain or IP address.

ODBC Administrator

This tool allows you to connect to and exchange data with ODBC-compliant data sources. ODBC, which stands for Open Database Connectivity, is a standard database protocol supported by most database systems such as FileMaker Pro, Oracle, MySQL, and PostgreSQL. You can use ODBC Administrator to add data sources, install new database drivers, trace calls to the ODBC API, and configure connection pooling.

Podcast Capture

Podcast Capture, which is new to Mac OS X Leopard, lets you easily record and distribute podcasts. The only caveat is that to use Podcast Capture, you need access to a system running Mac OS X Leopard Server with Podcast Producer. To learn more about Podcast Producer, see *http://www. apple.com/server/macosx/leopard/podcastproducer.html*.

RAID Utility

This utility lets you create a RAID array on your system. To use the RAID Utility, though, you'll need a RAID card installed in your Mac (which means you'll need a Mac Pro or an Xserve); you can't use the RAID Utility on a Mac laptop (MacBook, MacBook Pro, iBook, or Power-Book), iMac, or Mac mini.

System Profiler

This tool (formerly known as the Apple System Profiler) keeps track of the finer details about your system. Here, you can view information about your particular computer; the devices (e.g., Zip or Jaz drive, CD-ROM drives, etc.) and volumes (i.e., hard drives and partitions) connected to your Mac; and the frameworks, extensions, and applications on your Mac.

Terminal

The Terminal application is the command-line interface (CLI) to Mac OS X's Unix core.

VoiceOver Utility

The VoiceOver Utility provides you with an accessible interface for your Mac—allowing you to control your Mac with your keyboard instead of with a mouse—and provides screen-reader services for applications like Mail, Safari, and iChat, by which the computer speaks back messages, web pages, and chat sessions. VoiceOver is very powerful and—best of all—it's built right into the system.

X11

This is Apple's Mac OS X-compatible distribution of the X Window System. Since X11 is used primarily by long-time Unix users, it isn't installed by default, but it is available as one of the Custom options during the install.

NOTE

There are a few applications in the Utilities folder that some users may never use, including:

- Audio MIDI Setup
- Boot Camp Assistant
- Grapher
- Migration Assistant
- ODBC Administrator
- Podcast Capture
- RAID Utility
- X11

Deleting these utilities from your Mac will free up nearly 50 MB of space.

CHAPTER 6

Configuring Your Mac

You know that feeling you got when you first unpacked your Mac? You know, the anticipation you felt while you carefully opened the box—the rush of pulling all the clear plastic coverings off the power supply and untying the cables, plugging your precious Mac in, hitting the Power-On button, and finally hearing that "bwong" sound as your Mac started up? Well, that same anticipation is bound to hit you after installing Mac OS X Leopard. As you explore the system, you're certain to have lots of questions about setting things up and enabling certain checkboxes. This chapter should ease your transition and help you get your Leopard system set up just the way you want it. It presents helpful tips and tricks for configuring your Mac in a simple Q&A format. Each item starts with a simple "How do I…" question, followed by the steps you'll need to take to accomplish that task. For example:

Change the color depth of my display?
    System Preferences → Displays → Display → Colors → select from 256 Colors, Thousands, or Millions.

Can't find something you're looking for? Flip to the back of the book and look in the index to see whether your question is covered here or elsewhere in the book. The tasks are divided into the following sections:

- AirPort and Wireless Networking
- Customizing the System
- Files and Folders
- Fonts and Font Management

- .Mac
- Mail.app
- Maintenance and Troubleshooting
- Networking
- Obtaining Information About the System
- Printer Configuration and Printing
- Safari and the Internet
- Spotlight and Searching for Files

If you're new to Mac OS X, or if you just need to jog your memory because you can't quite remember the location of a particular setting, this is the place to start.

TIP

As you're configuring your Mac and switching back and forth among various System Preference panels, use ⌘-L to quickly switch back to System Preferences' main window.

AirPort and Wireless Networking

Here are some useful tips for working with a wireless system:

Add the AirPort menu extra to the menu bar?
System Preferences → Network → in the list of network services to the left, select AirPort → enable "Show AirPort status in menu bar."

Find the MAC address for my AirPort card?
System Preferences → Network → in the list of network services to the left, select AirPort → look next to AirPort ID.

Quickly switch to an AirPort network after disconnecting the Ethernet cable from my MacBook?
System Preferences → Network. At the bottom of the Services pane (to the left), click the Action button (the one that looks like a gear), and select "Set Service Order."

Drag the network service options (AirPort, Ethernet, Bluetooth, FireWire) around to place them in the order in which you're most likely to connect to them. For example, you might want to have AirPort on the top, followed by Ethernet, then Bluetooth and finally, FireWire. (Setting the Location pop up to Automatic should also do the trick.)

Share my modem or Ethernet connection with other AirPort-equipped Macs?

System Preferences → Sharing → in the list of Services (on the left), click the checkbox next to Internet Sharing → in the "Share your connection from" pop up, select the way your Mac is currently connected to the Internet (in this case, Ethernet) → in the "To computers using" list, enable AirPort.

Share a USB printer over an AirPort network?

If you have an AirPort Extreme or AirPort Express Base Station, all you need to do is connect the USB cable from the printer to the Base Station. The printer automatically becomes available to computers on the network.

If the printer is directly connected to your Mac, you'll need to enable Printer Sharing; there are two ways to do this:

- Go to System Preferences → Sharing → in the list of Services, click the checkbox next to Printer Sharing.

- Go to System Preferences → Print & Fax → select your printer in the list on the left → click the checkbox next to "Share these printers with other computers."

Customizing the System

The following are options you can use to customize the "Aqua look and feel" of your system:

Change the resolution of my display?
> System Preferences → Displays → Display → select a resolution that suits your needs.

Change my desktop image?
> System Preferences → Desktop & Screen Saver → Desktop.
>
> Control-click on the desktop itself and select Change Desktop Background from the context menu.
>
> If you have iPhoto, select one of the images in your iPhoto Library and click the Desktop button at the bottom of iPhoto's window.

Have the pictures on my desktop change automatically?
> System Preferences → Desktop & Screen Saver → Desktop; click the checkbox next to "Change picture" and select an interval from the pull-down menu.

Add a new background pattern and make it available to all users?
> Create or save the image to either the Abstract, Nature, or Solid Colors folder in */Library/Desktop Pictures*.

Change the double-click speed of my mouse?
> System Preferences → Keyboard & Mouse → Mouse or Trackpad panel → move the Double-Click Speed slider to a comfortable level.

Change the scrolling speed of my scrollwheel mouse?
> System Preferences → Keyboard & Mouse → Mouse pane → Scrolling Speed.

Change the settings on my MacBook's trackpad so it emulates mouse clicks?
> System Preferences → Keyboard & Mouse → Trackpad panel → Trackpad Gestures → select the checkboxes for the items you want. The items include "Use two fingers to scroll," "Zoom while holding" (a key; the Control key is the default), "Clicking," "Dragging," "Drag Lock" (tap again to release), and "Secondary Clicks" (which uses a combination of the trackpad and the mouse button).

Disable my MacBook Pro's trackpad when I'm using a Bluetooth mouse?

System Preferences → Keyboard & Mouse → Trackpad panel → Trackpad Options → select the checkbox for "Ignore trackpad when mouse is present."

Change the password for my user account?

System Preferences → Accounts → select your username → Password → Change Password.

Use the Password Assistant to help me choose a secure password?

System Preferences → Accounts → click on your username → Password → Change Password → enter your Old Password → click the "key" icon to the right of the New Password field. Clicking this pops open the Password Assistant shown in Figure 6-1. Select the Type of password you want to use and then move the Length slider right or left to get a longer or shorter password, respectively. When you've found a password you're comfortable with, jot it down somewhere and then close the window; the password is applied to your account.

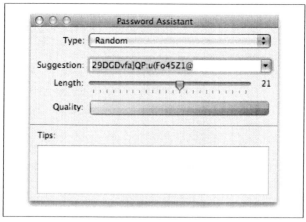

Figure 6-1. Leopard's Password Assistant helps you find a hard-to-guess password

Change the date/time?

System Preferences → Date & Time → Date & Time panel.

Specify how the date and time appear in the menu bar?

System Preferences → Date & Time → Clock → Show the date and time.

Specify the date and time settings for another country while I'm traveling?

To change the date: System Preferences → International → Formats → select a country from the Region pull-down menu.

To change the time: System Preferences → International → Formats → select a country from the Region pull-down menu.

Set up my Mac to tell me what time it is?

System Preferences → Date & Time → Clock → click the checkbox next to "Announce the time" → select how frequently you'd like your Mac to announce the time from the pop-up menu.

Use a network time server to set my clock's time?

System Preferences → Date & Time → Date & Time; enable the checkbox next to "Set date & time automatically" → select an NTP Server in the scroll list.

TIP

You must be connected to the Internet to use a network time server. One helpful hint is to use the network time server to set an accurate time for your system, then uncheck the "Set date & time automatically" box. This keeps your Mac from checking in with the server every time you restart the system.

Set my time zone?

System Preferences → Date & Time → Time Zone. When you do this, a map of the world appears; simply click your location on the map.

Change the name of my computer?

System Preferences → Sharing; enter the new name for your computer in the Computer Name text box.

Display the battery status for my MacBook in the menu bar?

System Preferences → Energy Saver → click Show Details → Options → select the checkbox next to "Show battery status in menu bar."

Display a volume control in the menu bar?

System Preferences → Sound → select the checkbox next to "Show volume in menu bar."

Quickly open the Sound preferences panel?

Hold down the Option key and press one of the volume keys (mute, or volume up/down) on your keyboard.

TIP

If you are using an Apple laptop (including the MacBook Pro, MacBook, PowerBook, and iBook), the volume keys on your laptop are as follows:

- Mute: F3
- Volume Down: F4
- Volume Up: F5

If you have an Apple Keyboard (wireless or USB) with a number pad, the volume keys are located across the top row of the number pad, to the right.

Set up my computer to check for updates to the system automatically?

System Preferences → Software Update → Scheduled Check → select the checkbox next to "Check for updates," and then select the frequency (Daily, Weekly, Monthly) from the pull-down menu.

Set up my computer to start an application automatically after I log in?

System Preferences → Accounts → click on your username → Login Items. Click the Add button (+) and then use the Finder sheet to select the application(s) you would like your Mac to start after you log in.

TIP

You can also drag an application icon from the Finder to the window in the Login Items pane within the Accounts panel.

Remove an application from my Login Items list?

System Preferences → Accounts → click on your username → Login Items → select the application name you want to remove from the list → either click the minus button (–) or press the Delete key on your keyboard.

Adjust the amount of time my system must be idle before the screensaver kicks in?

System Preferences → Desktop & Screen Saver → Screen Saver → adjust the slider next to "Start screen saver."

Quickly activate my screensaver when I know I'll be away from my desk for a while?

System Preferences → Desktop & Screen Saver → Screen Saver → click the Hot Corners button at the bottom of the window → use the pop-up menus to mark one of the corners of your screen for "Start Screen Saver." Now when you want to enable the screensaver, all you need to do is move the mouse to that corner of the screen.

Protect my system from prying eyes while I'm away from my computer?

System Preferences → Security → General → enable the checkbox next to "Require password to wake this computer from sleep or screen saver."

Change the background of a Finder window to a different color or to an image?

Finder → View → as Icons, then use View → Show View Options (⌘-J); select either Color or Picture from the list of Background options.

TIP

You cannot change the background of the Finder window if the View is set to "as Columns" or "as Cover Flow."

Set up my computer to start up or shut down at the same time every day?

System Preferences → Energy Saver → click the Schedule button.

Set up my computer to restart automatically after a power failure?

System Preferences → Energy Saver → Show Details → Options → enable the checkbox next to "Restart automatically after a power failure."

TIP

The benefit of having a Mac laptop (such as a MacBook or a MacBook Pro) is that if you lose power when your Mac is plugged in, the internal battery automatically kicks in. However, if the power is still out when your battery is running low, then you're in a pickle.

Enable full keyboard access so I can navigate my system and select menu items without using a mouse?

System Preferences → Keyboard & Mouse → Keyboard Shortcuts → Full keyboard access → click the radio button for "All controls."

Use the RSS screensaver?

To change Leopard's default screensaver so that it uses the RSS feed, follow these steps:

1. Open System Preferences and select the Desktop & Screen Saver panel.

2. Click the Screen Saver tab.

3. In the list of available Screen Savers to the left, select "RSS Visualizer."

4. After selecting RSS Visualizer, you'll see a demo of the RSS screen saver in the display to the right.

By default, Leopard's RSS screen saver calls up news items from Apple's Hot News RSS feed. If you want to select a different site:

1. Click the Options button.

2. A sheet slides out, displaying a list of RSS feeds that you can choose from.

3. Select a feed, or type in the URL for a feed from another site, such as Digg (*http://www.digg.com/rss/index.xml*).

4. Click Done.

5. To see what the screensaver looks like, click the Test button.

Now when the screensaver jumps into action, you'll see news items fed to you from Digg.

TIP

Your computer must have a Quartz Extreme-compatible graphics card for the RSS Visualizer to even appear in the list. If you don't see this item in the list of available screensavers, your Mac won't be able to use this feature.

Register my license number for QuickTime Pro?

System Preferences → QuickTime → click the Registration button and enter your license number.

Set a Keyboard Shortcut for Sleep?

If you want to add a keyboard shortcut for Sleep (⬤ → Sleep), you can do so by taking the following steps:

1. Launch System Preferences by clicking its icon in the Dock.

2. Select the Keyboard & Mouse preference panel.

3. Select the Keyboard Shortcuts tab.

4. Beneath the list of keyboard shortcuts in the middle of the window, you'll see plus (+) and minus (–) sign buttons. Click the plus button to add an item to the list.

5. In the sheet that slides out of the window's title bar, select Finder from the Application pop-up menu.

6. In the Menu Title field, type in "Sleep." This tells the Finder to look for this menu item.

7. Tab down to the Keyboard Shortcut field and create a keyboard shortcut that works for you. For example, you could set the keyboard shortcut for Sleep to Control-Option-⌘-S.

8. Quit System Preferences (⌘-Q).

9. Because you've made changes, you'll need to restart the Finder. To do this, go to ⬤ → Force Quit (Option-⌘-Esc) to open the Force Quit window.

10. Select the Finder and then click the Relaunch button. After clicking the Relaunch button, you'll be prompted with an alert dialog box asking whether you really want to relaunch the Finder. Since this is what you want to do, click on the Relaunch button in the sheet. After a brief pause, your Dock quits and restarts.

11. Close the Force Quit window by clicking on the red close-window button in the window's title bar.

12. Now if you go to the Apple menu, you'll see that the keyboard shortcut you've added for Sleep shows up in the menu. Give it a try!

Files and Folders

The following are options to use with files and folders:

Create a new folder?
> Control-click → New Folder (in the Finder or on the desktop).
>
> Shift-⌘-N.

TIP

In earlier versions of the Mac OS, ⌘-N was used to create new folders; now, ⌘-N is used for opening a new Finder window.

Rename a file or folder?
> Click once on the icon and then click once on the name of the file to highlight it (or press Return). Type in the new name for the file or folder and hit Return to accept the new name.
>
> Click on the icon, then use ⌘-I to open the Get Info window. Click on the disclosure triangle next to Name & Extension and enter the new file or directory name.

Use Smart Folders to organize my files?
> One of the things you'll notice with Leopard is that Smart Folders are everywhere—and that's a good thing. Beyond using Smart Folders to organize your music in iTunes, you can now use them to help you organize files with the Finder. For example, let's say you're a photographer and that you shoot with more than one type of digital

camera, but you want to find only the shots you've taken with your Canon 30D. To create a Smart Folder to find these photographs, do the following:

1. Switch to the Finder and select File → New Smart Folder (Option-⌘-N); the Finder window changes slightly, giving you options for setting the Smart Folder's filtering criteria.

2. Beneath the Finder's toolbar, you'll see a silver bar with buttons that say This Mac, and the short username for your account. By default, this is set to This Mac, but since you don't want system files included, select your username so the Smart Folder looks only in your Home folder and its subfolders (such as Documents, Movies, etc.). There's also a Save button to the far right, but don't click on that just yet.

3. Next to the Save button, click the Add (+) button to start adding search criteria for the Smart Folder.

4. The first pop-up menu of the next row is labeled "What"; click that and select Other at the bottom of the list.

5. In the sheet that slides down, you'll see a list of options you can add to that pop-up menu. The sheet also has a Search field, which helps you quickly find the item you're looking for. Since you want to search for images created by a particular camera (a device), type "device" into the Search field. You will see three options, but you'll want the first two: "Device make" and "Device model." Click the checkboxes at the far right to add those options to the pop-up menu, and then click OK.

6. Now the pop-up menu is set to "Device make." Leave the pop-up menu set to that, and then in the text field next to the "matches" pop up, type in "Canon."

7. Click the Add (+) button at the far right of that row.

8. In the next row, select "Device model," and in the text field next to "matches," type in "30D."

9. Now click the Save button; you'll be asked to enter a name for the folder, so give it a name such as "Shot with the 30D."

10. Leave the Where pop up set to Saved Searches, and leave the Add To Sidebar checkbox checked.

11. Click the Save button.

The new Smart Folder appears in the Finder's Sidebar and gives you quick access to the photos you've taken with your Canon 30D. If you are using multiple cameras, such as a Canon 5D or those taken with your iPhone, consider setting up Smart Folders for those as well.

Create a Burn Folder to help me back up important files?

In the Finder, go to the location where you want to create the Burn Folder and follow these steps:

1. From the File menu, select New Burn Folder.

NOTE

There is no keyboard shortcut for creating a new Burn Folder. However, if you follow the same steps and principles as for adding a keyboard shortcut for the Sleep item, you can quickly create a shortcut for New Burn Folder in the same way.

---

2. Change the name of the folder from "Burn Folder" to some other name appropriate for your needs (such as "Files2Burn").

3. Drag and drop any items (files, folders, applications, whatever) to the Burn Folder. Mac OS X places an alias of these items inside the Burn Folder.

To actually burn a CD from the Burn Folder:

1. Select the Burn Folder in the Finder. When you do this, you'll notice that a grayish-black bar appears in the Finder's view, with a Burn button at its right edge.

2. When you click the Burn button, you are asked to insert a blank CD; go ahead and do so.

3. If the blank CD you've inserted is accepted by the drive, another window pops up, allowing you to assign a name to the disc you're about to burn. By default, the name is set to that of the Burn Folder (in this case, Files2Burn).

4. To burn the files to CD, click the Burn button.

TIP

While you can drag a Smart Folder from your Saved Searches folder (~/Library/Saved Searches) to a Burn Folder to create an alias of it there, the files found by the Smart Folder's search criteria unfortunately don't get brought along. When you burn a copy of the Burn Folder, you're burning a copy of the *.savedSearch* file and not, as you may have hoped, the files found by the Smart Folder's search criteria.

Change the program associated with a particular extension?
Click on a file and then use ⌘-I or File → Get Info. Click on the disclosure triangle next to "Open with" and either select one of the applications from the pull-down menu or choose Other to select a different program. If you want to specify the application you selected as the default for opening files with that particular extension, click Change All; otherwise, close the Info window to save the changes.

Change the permissions for a file or directory?

Click on a file or directory and then use ⌘-I or File → Get Info. Click on the disclosure triangle next to Sharing & Permissions to change the access for Owner, Staff, and Everyone. Before you can change the permissions, however, you first need to authenticate by clicking on the Lock icon in the lower-right corner of the Get Info window.

Copy a file to the Desktop instead of moving it or creating a shortcut?

Select the file, then Option-drag the icon to the desktop (notice that a plus sign appears next to the pointer in a green bubble) and release the mouse button.

In the Finder, select the file → Edit → Copy *filename* → click on the Home icon in the Finder's sidebar → double-click on the Desktop icon → Edit → Paste item.

Find out where an open document is saved on my system?

Command-click on the name of the document in the title bar. A menu drops down from the name of the file showing you where the file is located. If you go down to one of the folders in that menu and release the mouse, a Finder window opens for that location.

Create a disk image?

To create a disk image, follow these steps:

1. Launch Disk Utility (*/Application/Utilities*).

2. In the menu bar, select File → New → Blank Disk Image, or click on the New Image button in Disk Utility's toolbar.

3. In the Save As field, enter a name for the disk image.

4. From the Where pop-up menu, select the location where you'd like to save the disk image.

5. Type in a Volume Name, and then set the Volume Size, Volume Format, Encryption method, Partitions, and Image Format from their respective pop-up menus.

6. Click the Create button to create the disk image; the disk image file (with a *.dmg* file extension) is saved in the location you selected, and the image itself is mounted on your desktop.

7. Drag and drop the items you would like included in the disk image into the image's Finder window; a copy of the file is placed in the open disk image.

8. When you're finished, eject the disk image by either clicking the Eject icon next to its name in the Finder's Sidebar or selecting the disk image and selecting File → Eject *image_name* (⌘-E) to complete the process.

To create a disk image from a folder so you can burn and back it up to a CD:

1. Launch Disk Utility (*/Applications/Utilities*).

2. In the menu bar, select File → New → Disk Image from Folder (Shift-⌘-N).

3. The "Select Folder to Image" window pops open; use this window just as you would a Finder window and select the folder you want to image; click the Image button.

4. The name of the folder appears in the Save As field; if you want to change this, enter a new name for the image you want to create.

5. From the Where pop-up menu, select the location where you'd like to save the disk image.

6. Select the Image Format and Encryption Type from their respective pop-up menus.

7. Click the Save button to create the disk image.

Burn a disk image to CD?

To burn a disk image you've created (see the previous descriptions):

1. Select the disk image in the Finder.

2. In the menu bar, select File → Burn *image name* to Disc.

3. Insert a blank CD.

4. Click Burn.

Display the contents of a shared folder on another volume in my network?

Finder → select the volume in the Shared section of the Finder's Sidebar → select the folder.

Move a file to the Trash from the Finder?

Select the file and press ⌘-Delete.

Make the Trash stop asking me whether I'm sure I want to delete every file?

Finder → Preferences → Advanced → uncheck the option next to "Show warning before emptying the Trash."

Empty the Trash of locked items?

Shift-Option-⌘-Delete. The addition of the Option key forces the deletion of Trash contents.

Give a file or folder a custom icon?

Open an image file and copy it with ⌘-C. Select the icon → File → Get Info (or ⌘-I). Select the file icon in the General section and then paste in (⌘-V) the new image.

TIP

The proper image size for an icon is 512×512 pixels. This used to be 128×128, but with Apple's push for resolution independence, larger icons will soon be a requirement, so it's better to start now.

Fonts and Font Management

Use the following options for fonts and font management:

Share fonts with other users on my system?
> If you're the administrator, move the font you'd like to share from your */Users/username/Library/Fonts* directory to */Library/Fonts*.

Where can I store new fonts I've purchased or downloaded from the Internet?
> Save them to */Users/username/Library/Fonts* for your personal use, or save them to */Library/Fonts* to allow everyone on the system access to them.

Why aren't my bitmap fonts working?
> Mac OS X doesn't support bitmapped fonts; it supports only TrueType, OpenType, and PostScript Level 1 fonts.

What does the .dfont extension on some of my Mac OS X fonts mean?
> The extension stands for Data Fork TrueType Font. Basically, it just tells you the font is a TrueType font.

Turn off font antialiasing?
> You can't, but you can adjust the minimum font size so that it's affected by font smoothing in System Preferences → Appearance → "Turn off text smoothing for font sizes *X* and smaller" (4 points is the default setting).

Create a Font Collection?
> Launch the Font Book application (*/Applications*) and follow these steps:
>
> 1. Select File → New Collection (⌘-N) from the menu bar.
>
> 2. A new collection named New-0 (or some other number) appears in the Collection column; type in a different name (such as BookFonts) and press Return.

---

3. At the top of the Collection column, select All Fonts to see a list of the installed fonts in the Font column.

4. Drag the fonts you want from the Font column and drop them onto the name of the collection you've created.

TIP

You can ⌘-click on the font names to select multiple fonts at one time before dragging them to your Font Collection.

Where are my Font Collections stored?
/Users/username/Library/FontCollections. If you want to share a collection with another user, place a copy of the collection in the Shared folder. All Font Collections have a *.collection* file extension.

.Mac

Set up a .Mac account?
System Preferences → .Mac → Account → Learn More. (You must be connected to the Internet to set up a .Mac account.)

Find out how much space I have available on my iDisk?
System Preferences → .Mac → iDisk.

Require a password from other users before they can access my iDisk's Public folder?
System Preferences → .Mac → iDisk → enable the checkbox next to "Use a Password to Protect your Public Folder" and then click on the Password button to set a password.

Create a local copy of my iDisk on my hard drive so I can back it up?

System Preferences → .Mac → iDisk → click the Start button in the iDisk Sync section → select Automatically or Manually to indicate how you want to synchronize your iDisk with your local copy.

Find out how many days are remaining on my .Mac membership before I have to renew?

System Preferences → .Mac → Account.

Mount my iDisk?

Click the iDisk icon in the Finder's Sidebar.

From the Finder's menu bar, select Go → iDisk → My iDisk.

From the Finder, use the keyboard shortcut Shift-⌘-I.

Unmount my iDisk?

Select the iDisk icon in the Finder's Sidebar and select File → Eject.

Drag your iDisk's icon from the desktop to the Trash.

Synchronize data on my Mac with my .Mac account?

System Preferences → .Mac → Sync → select the items you want to synchronize → click Sync Now.

Synchronize my Address Book contacts from my MacBook Pro to my iMac?

On the MacBook Pro, select System Preferences → .Mac → Sync → select the items you want to synchronize → click Sync Now. Go to your iMac and make sure the .Mac Account pane is set up to use your .Mac account, then go to the Advanced pane and click "Register this Computer." This registers the iMac with the .Mac synchronization server; once it's registered, go back to the Sync pane on the iMac and click Sync Now.

Use Leopard's "Back To My Mac" feature?

The key to using "Back To My Mac" (or B2MM, for short) is that you need to have two Macs running Mac OS X Leopard, since this is a new-to-Leopard feature. The Macs also need to be configured with the same .Mac member name and password. Once B2MM is set up on both computers, you'll need to turn on the Sharing Services in the Sharing preference panel. For example, if you want to swap files, enable File Sharing, or if you want to be able to log in remotely, enable Remote Login. The other computer will show up in the Shared section of the Finder's Sidebar.

Mail.app

Everyone uses email these days, even my parents. Here are some tips to help you work with Leopard's new Mail application:

Enable junk mail filtering?

Mail → Preferences (⌘-,) → Junk Mail → turn on "Enable junk mail filtering."

Set up my mailbox to sort junk mail into a separate mailbox so spam messages don't clutter my inbox?

Mail → Preferences (⌘-,) → Junk Mail → turn on "Enable junk mail filtering." In the "When junk mail arrives" section, turn on "Move it to the Junk mailbox (Automatic)."

Get rid of the junk mail I've received?

Mailbox → Erase Junk Mail (Option-⌘-J).

Empty Mail's trash?

Mailbox → Erase Deleted Messages → In All Accounts (⌘-K).

View messages with similar subject lines as a thread?

Select the mailbox → View → Organize by Thread.

Synchronize messages with my .Mac account?
   Mailbox → Synchronize Account.

Change Mail so the messages I write use plain text?
   Mail → Preferences (⌘-,) → Composing → Composing:
   Message Format → select Plain Text from the pop-up
   menu.

Create Smart Mailboxes to organize my messages in Mail.app?
   Regardless of whether you use your Mac at work or at
   home, chances are you get a lot of email every day. And
   what better way to help you organize your email than
   with Mail.app's new Smart Mailbox feature? Smart Mailboxes can be used for anything from sorting emails from
   your boss into a different folder than emails from your
   friends, to sorting your messages based on the time they
   were received.

   For example, let's say you want to create two Smart
   Mailboxes, one for email messages you've received
   today, and another for messages you've received this
   week. To create these Smart Mailboxes, follow these
   steps:

   1. Launch *Mail.app* by clicking its icon in the Dock or
      by double-clicking its icon in the Finder.

   2. From the Mailbox menu, select the New Smart Mail-
      box item.

   3. In the Smart Mailbox Name field, type in "Today's
      Email."

   4. Change the From pop up to Date Received, and leave
      the second pop up set to "is today."

   5. Click OK.

   This creates a Smart Mailbox that, when selected, only
   displays the Inbox messages that came in today. Now
   create another Smart Mailbox for email received this
   week:

1. From the Mailbox menu, select the New Smart Mailbox item.

2. In the Smart Mailbox Name field, type in "This Week."

3. Change the From pop up to Date Received.

4. Change the second pop up from "is today" to "is this week."

5. Click OK.

The possibilities are limitless, so use your imagination and create Smart Mailboxes to automatically sort and sift your messages to your heart's content!

Maintenance and Troubleshooting

The following settings deal with maintenance and trouble-shooting issues:

Force quit an application that's stuck?
> Option-⌘-Escape opens a window that shows all the running applications. Select the troublesome application and click the Force Quit button.
>
> Option-click the application's icon in the Dock. In the contextual menu that appears, select the Force Quit option.
>
> Activity Monitor (*/Applications/Utilities*) → select the process causing the problem → Processes → click Quit Process in the toolbar.

Restart my system if it's completely frozen?
> Hold down the Shift-Option-⌘ keys and press the Power-On button.

Fix a disk that won't mount?
> Disk Utility (*/Applications/Utilities*) → select the disk that won't mount → First Aid.

Partition a new hard drive?

Applications → Utilities → Disk Utility → select the new drive → Partition.

TIP

You cannot partition an active drive for a system you're logged into. If you want to partition the only hard drive on your Mac, you'll need to insert your Mac OS X Leopard Install DVD, and restart your Mac holding down the C key. Then select Disk Utility from the Utilities menu.

It's also worth noting that partitioning a drive erases all of the data on it. So, if you're going to partition an existing drive, you should back up all of the data on it first (now's a good time to start using Time Machine for the backup).

Erase a CD-RW disc or hard drive?

Disk Utility (*/Applications/Utilities*) → select the CD or disk → Erase.

Create a redundant array of independent disks (RAID) for my system?

Disk Utility (*/Applications/Utilities*) → select the drives → RAID.

There is a question mark icon in the Dock. What is this?

A question mark icon in the Dock or in one of the toolbars means that the application, folder, or file that the original icon related to has been deleted from your system. Just drag the question mark icon away from the Dock or toolbar to make it disappear.

I have a quad-core Mac Pro. Can I see how efficiently the processors are distributing the workload?

Activity Monitor (*/Applications/Utilities*) → CPU; each processor has its own meter bar.

View a log of software updates?

System Preferences → Software Update → Show Log.

How do I connect an external monitor or projector to my Mac-Book Pro without restarting it?

Select → Sleep to put your laptop to sleep, plug in and turn on the display, and then hit the Escape key to wake your system and the display. You can then use the Displays preference panel (System Preferences → Displays) to turn display mirroring on or off as needed.

Networking

The following settings aid with networking settings:

Find the media access control (MAC) address for my Ethernet card?

System Preferences → Network → select Ethernet in the left pane → click the Advanced button → select the Ethernet tab → look next to Ethernet ID for your MAC address.

Configure my system to connect to an Ethernet network?

Go to System Preferences → Network and follow these steps:

1. Select Ethernet in the left pane.

2. From the Configure pull-down menu, select Using DHCP if your IP address is assigned dynamically, or Manually if your machine has a fixed IP address. (In most cases, particularly if you have a broadband Internet connection at home, your IP address is assigned via DHCP.)

3. If you're on an AppleTalk network, click the Advanced button, choose the AppleTalk tab, select the Make AppleTalk Active option, and select your AppleTalk Zone (if any).

4. Click Apply.

Change my computer's name from my full name to something else?

System Preferences → Sharing; enter the new name in the Computer Name text box. Your computer's name, which is also used for Bonjour networking, has a *.local* extension; for example, *MacLeopard.local*.

Find out the speed of my network connection?

Network Utility (*/Applications/Utilities*) → Info panel; look next to Link Speed in the Interface Information section.

Find out what's taking a site so long to respond?

Network Utility (*/Applications/Utilities*) → Ping panel → enter the network address for the location (e.g., *http:// www.apple.com* or *17.112.152.32*).

Trace the route taken to connect to a web page?

Network Utility (*/Applications/Utilities*) → Traceroute panel → enter the hostname for the location.

Allow others access to my computer so they can retrieve files I make available to them?

System Preferences → Sharing → Services → click "File Sharing" → click Start. This turns on File Sharing, which gives others access to your Public folder (*/Users/ username/Public*). The Public folder is read-only, which means that other people can only view or copy files in that folder; they cannot save files to that folder.

Allow my coworkers to place files on my computer without giving them access to the rest of my system?

With Personal File Sharing turned on (see previous item), other users can place files, folders, or even applications in your Drop Box, located within the Public folder (*/Users/ username/Public/Drop Box*).

View what's inside someone else's iDisk Public folder?

Go → Connect to Server. At the bottom of the dialog box, type **http://idisk.mac.com/***membername***/Public**. Click Connect or press Return; the Public iDisk image mounts on your desktop.

Connect to a networked drive?

Look in the Shared section of the Finder's Sidebar to see whether the drive shows up there.

Go → Connect to Server (⌘-K).

If the server to which you want to connect is part of your local area network (LAN), click on the Local icon in the left pane and select the server name to the right. If the server to which you want to connect is part of your local AppleTalk network, click the AppleTalk Network icon in the left pane and select the server or computer name to the right.

Connect to a Windows server?

If you need to connect to a Windows server, you must specify the address in the text box as follows:

smb://hostname/sharename

After clicking the Connect button, you are asked to supply the domain to which you wish to connect and your username and password.

You can speed up this process by supplying the domain and your username, as follows:

smb://*domain*;*username*@*hostname*/*sharename*

where *domain* is the NT domain name, *username* is the name you use to connect to that domain, and *hostname* and *sharename* are the server name and shared directory that you have or want access to. Now when you click the Connect button, all you need to do is enter your password (if one is required), and the networked drive mounts on your desktop.

TIP

Before pressing the Connect button, press the Add button (+) to add the server to your list of Favorites. This saves you time in the future if you frequently need to connect to the same drive because you won't have to enter its address again.

Obtaining Information About the System

Use the following if you need to obtain system information:

Find out how much disk space I have left?
Launch the Finder and look in the thin bar just below the toolbar. You will see something that says how many items are in that directory and how much space is available on your hard drive.

Find out how much memory I have?
 → About This Mac.

Find out what version of Mac OS X I'm running?
 → About This Mac.

 → About This Mac; click on the version number (e.g., 10.5) to reveal the build number (e.g., 9A559).

System Profiler (*/Applications/Utilities*) → Contents → select Software to see the exact build of Mac OS X.

Find out what processor my Mac has?

 → About This Mac.

System Profiler (*/Applications/Utilities*) → Contents → select Hardware.

Find out what type of cache I have and how big it is?

System Profiler (*/Applications/Utilities*) → Contents → select Hardware → look for L2 and/or L3 Cache items, to the right.

Find out whether a drive is formatted with Journaled HFS+?

System Profiler (*/Applications/Utilities*) → Contents → select your drive type (such as Serial-ATA) → in the right pane, scroll down and look next to File System.

Disk Utility (*/Applications/Utilities*) → select the drive or partition in the left column → click on the Info button → the File System type should read Mac OS Extended (Journaled).

Find out which programs (or processes) are running?

Activity Monitor (*/Applications/Utilities*).

Display the status of the computer's used and free memory?

Activity Monitor (/Applications/Utilities) → System Memory → the far right column shows how much memory is in use or is free.

View the hardware connected to my system?

System Profiler (*/Applications/Utilities*). This information can be found in the Hardware section.

Create a profile of my Mac with System Profiler?

If you need to call AppleCare for assistance, it's always good to have a recent copy of your system profile on hand. Your system profile, which is created with System Profiler (*/Applications/Utilities*), provides a detailed list of information about your Mac's hardware configuration (type of hard drive, amount of RAM, and so on), as well as the applications, extensions, and other important system logs for your computer.

To create a profile of your Mac, follow these steps:

1. In the Finder, go to your Applications → Utilities folder (or use the keyboard shortcut Shift-⌘-U to quickly open the Utilities folder in the Finder).

2. Launch the System Profiler.

3. From the File menu, select Save.

4. In the field at the top of the sheet that appears, give your system profile a name, such as *chucktoporek_sysprofile*.

5. In the Where pop up, the location of your Mac's profile is set to your Documents folder. Either leave this as it is or select another folder of your choice.

6. In the File Format pop up, leave the type set to System Profiler 4.0 (XML).

7. Click Save.

8. Now if you ever need to file a bug with Apple or if you need a copy of your system profile to send to AppleCare, you'll have one on hand.

TIP

It's a good idea to create a copy of your system profile every week or so, just to be safe.

Printer Configuration and Printing

Use these options for printer configuration and printing:

Configure a printer?
System Preferences → Print & Fax → in the window that appears, select your printer type and click the Add button.

View the jobs in the print queue?
System Preferences → Print & Fax → double-click on the name of the printer to see the print queue.

Cancel a print job?
> System Preferences → Print & Fax → double-click on the printer name → click on the name of the print job → click the Delete button.

Halt a print job?
> System Preferences → Print & Fax → double-click on the printer name → click on the name of the print job → click on the Hold button. (Click on the Resume button to start the job where it left off.)

Share my printer with another user?
> System Preferences → Sharing → Services → turn on the checkbox next to Printer Sharing.

Spotlight and Searching for Files

The following will help you search for and locate files:

Find a file if I don't know its name?
> Use ⌘-Space to open Spotlight's Search field; enter a keyword in the field.
>
> Finder → enter a keyword in the toolbar Search field.
>
> Finder → File → Find (⌘-F).

Find a file if I can't remember where I saved it?
> Hit ⌘-Space to open Spotlight's Search field → enter the name of the file → select the file in the list of items Spotlight finds; the file opens in its default application.

Change the shortcut key for opening Spotlight's Search field?
> System Preferences → Spotlight → Spotlight menu keyboard shortcut → click the pop-up menu to select one of the F keys (F1–F12), or type in your own shortcut (for example, Control-⌘-Space, which appears in the menu as ^⌘ Space).

Change the order in which Spotlight displays its search results?
    System Preferences → Spotlight → Search Results → select
    and drag categories in the order you prefer; for example,
    select and drag Documents to the top of the list.

Stop Spotlight from searching through my music files?
    System Preferences → Spotlight → Privacy → click the
    Add (+) button → select your Music folder → click
    Choose to add your Music folder to the list.

Safari and the Internet

Use the following settings according to your Internet, Web,
and email usage:

Change Safari's default home page?
    Safari → Preferences (⌘-,) → General → "Home page" →
    enter a different URL in this field (for example, *http://
    www.appleinsider.com*).

Enable tabbed viewing in Safari?
    Safari → View → Show Tab Bar (Shift-⌘-T).

*Set up Safari so it remembers passwords for web sites I'm
required to log in to?*
    Safari → Preferences (⌘-,) → AutoFill → click the check-
    box next to "Usernames and passwords."

*Change my default RSS news reader from Safari to
NetNewsWire?*
    Safari → Preferences (⌘-,) → RSS → Default RSS Reader →
    select NetNewsWire from the pop up.

Block pop-up windows from appearing when I'm surfing the Web?

Safari → Preferences (⌘-,) → Security → click the checkbox next to "Block pop-up windows."

Set up Safari to check spelling for me when I'm using Gmail or .Mac's web-based Mail?

Edit → Spelling and Grammar → Check Spelling While Typing.

Set up Safari so it doesn't keep track of my history?

Safari → Private Browsing (read the disclaimer window that pops up before clicking OK).

Turn on web sharing?

System Preferences → Sharing → Services pane → enable the checkbox next to Web Sharing to start this service. Enabling this service allows others to access your Sites folder (*/Users/username/Sites*) from the Internet. To learn more about Web Sharing, point your default browser to */Users/username/Sites/index.html*. The address for your personal web site is *http://yourIPAddress/~yourshortusername/*.

Listen to an Internet radio station?

Dock → iTunes → Radio. When you click the Radio option in the Source pane to the left, the right pane changes to show you a list of different music genres from which to choose. Click the disclosure triangle next to a music type to reveal the available stations.

Use my own stylesheet for viewing web pages in Safari?

Safari → Preferences (⌘-,) → Advanced → Style Sheet → Other → locate and select the Cascading Style Sheet (CSS) you want to apply.

Create shortcuts on my desktop for web sites I visit often or email addresses I use frequently?

Open the TextEdit application, enter a URL (such as *http://developer.apple.com*) or an email address (e.g., *chuckdude@mac.com*), then triple-click on the address to select the entire line and drag it to your desktop; this creates an icon on your desktop for whatever you drag there. When you double-click on the icon, your default web browser opens that URL, or your email client creates a new message window with the address specified by the shortcut.

Empty Safari's cache?

Safari → Empty Safari's Cache (Option-⌘-E).

Clear Safari's History file?

History → Clear History.

Mark a web page for SnapBack?

History → Mark Page for SnapBack (Option-⌘-K).

CHAPTER 7

Special Characters

Included with Mac O X is the Keyboard Viewer application, which is a keyboard widget that allows you to see which character is created by applying the Shift, Option, or Shift-Option keys to any key on the keyboard. To enable Keyboard Viewer, go to System Preferences → International → Input Menu, and select the checkbox next to Keyboard Viewer. The Input menu appears in the menu bar; to launch the Keyboard Viewer, simply select this item from the Input menu.

While this application might seem useful, it can be a hassle to launch another app just to create one character and copy and paste it into another program. Fortunately, the Mac OS is able (through one of its least-known and most infrequently used features) to give you the same functionality within any application, making Keyboard Viewer unnecessary if you know what you're doing.

Table 7-1 lists the special characters. Keep in mind that this doesn't work for all font types, and some fonts, such as Symbol, Wingdings, and Zapf Dingbats, create an entirely different set of characters or symbols. For example, to create the symbol for the Command key (⌘), you need to switch the font to Wingdings and type a lowercase z.

Table 7-1. Special characters and their key mappings

Normal	Shift	Option	Shift-Option
1	!	¡	/
2	@	™	€
3	#	£	‹
4	$	¢	›
5	%	∞	fi
6	^	§	fl
7	&	¶	‡
8	*	•	°
9	(	ª	·
0	)	º	‚
`	~	Grave (`)a	`
- (hyphen)	_ (underscore)	– (en-dash)	— (em-dash)
=	+	≠	±
[	{	"	"
]	}	"	'
\	|	«	»
;	:	…	Ú
'	"	æ	Æ
,	<	≤	¯
.	>	≥	˘
/	?	÷	¿
a	A	å	Å
b	B	∫	ı
c	C	ç	Ç
d	D	∂	Î
e	E	Acute (´)a	´
f	F	ƒ	Ï

Table 7-1. Special characters and their key mappings (continued)

Normal	Shift	Option	Shift-Option
g	G	©	"
h	H	˙	Ó
i	I	Circumflex (ˆ)[a]	ˆ
j	J	Δ	Ô
k	K	°	
l	L	¬	Ò
m	M	µ	Â
n	N	Tilde (˜)[a]	˜
o	O	ø	Ø
p	P	π	TM
q	Q	œ	Œ
r	R	®	‰
s	S	ß	Í
t	T	†	ˇ
u	U	Umlaut (¨)[a]	¨
v	V	√	◊
w	W	Σ	„
x	X	≈	˛
y	Y	¥	Á
z	Z	Ω	˒

[a] To apply this accent, you must press another key after invoking the Option-key command. See Table 7-2.

One thing you might have noticed in Table 7-1 is that when the Option key is used with certain letters, it doesn't necessarily create a special character right away; you need to press another character key to apply the accent. When used with the ` (backtick), E, I, N, and U characters, the Option key creates the accented characters shown in Table 7-2.

Table 7-2. Option-key commands for creating accented characters

Key	Option-`	Option-E	Option-I	Option-N	Option-U
a	à	á	â	ã	ä
Shift-A	À	Á	Â	Ã	Ä
e	è	é	ê	ē	ë
Shift-E	È	É	Ê	Ē	Ë
i	ì	í	î	ĩ	ï
Shift-I	Ì	Í	Î	Ĩ	Ï
o	ò	ó	ô	õ	ö
Shift-O	Ò	Ó	Ô	Õ	Ö
u	ù	ú	Û	ū	ü
Shift-U	Ù	Ú	û	Ū	Ü

For example, to create the acute-accented *e*s in the word "résumé," you would type Option-E and then press the E key. If you want an uppercase acute-accented E (É), press Option-E and then Shift-E. Try this out with various characters in different fonts to see what sort of characters you can create.

Index

We'd like to hear your suggestions for improving our indexes. Send email to
index@oreilly.com.

mouse, using, 160
network settings, 135
Bluetooth Sharing, 44
Bonjour, 151
Boot Camp, 18
Boot Camp Assistant, 150
BSD flat files, 151
Burn Folders, creating
for file backup, 169
options for, 99
using Finder Action menu, 90
Business Widget, 104

C

cache, identifying size and
type, 185
Calculator, 104, 142
CalDAV-enabled server, 144
calendars (see iCal)
cartoons (Big Cartoon
Database), 111
CDs & DVDs preference
panel, 131
characters, special (see special
characters)
Chess, 142
Clear Menu option (Recent
Items), 56
Clock Widgets, 106
color labels, 93
ColorSync Utility, 151
Combo Updates, 36
Command key symbol, 191
computer name, changing, 162,
182
Console, 151
Copy
Finder Action menu item, 93
keyboard shortcut, 52
Core Animation, 2
Cover Flow, 4
CRT displays, 132
Cut command, keyboard
shortcut, 52

D

Dashboard, 103–113, 142
documentation, 107
finding more Widgets, 107
installing Widgets, 110
managing Widgets, 109
preinstalled Widgets, 104–106
viewing, 107–109
keyboard shortcuts, 108
Widget preferences, 111–113
Dashboard & Exposé preference
panel, 103
Date & Time preference
panel, 137
customizing system
information, 161
password protecting, 45
dates and times
scheduling startup or
shutdown, 164
World Clock Widget, 106
Desktop folder, 21
Dictionary, 143
Parental Controls, 33
Dictionary/Thesaurus/Apple
Widget, 104
DigitalColor Meter, 151
Directory, 151
Directory Utility, 151
Discovery Services, 151
disk image, creating, 171
disk space, 184
Disk Utility, 152
creating secure disk image of
Keychains folder, 39
Displays preference panel, 131
changing resolution, 159
Dock, 55, 69–78
adding programs, 76
animation of opening
application icons, 76
changing location on
screen, 76
changing preferences, 75

M